EXIT RAMP

Escaping the Besetting Sin of Sexual Addiction

John Allen Brown

INFINITY PUBLISHING

ISBN 978-0-7414-6939-7

Printed in the United States of America

Published July 2013

INFINITY PUBLISHING
1094 New DeHaven Street, Suite 100
West Conshohocken, PA 19428-2713
Toll-free (877) BUY BOOK
Local Phone (610) 941-9999
Fax (610) 941-9959
Info@buybooksontheweb.com
www.buybooksontheweb.com

DEDICATION

This book is dedicated to my son, John David. You are a priceless jewel of God's grace in my soul. My prayer is that you will learn from my mistakes in such a manner that you never follow the errant path I once chose.

John Allen Brown
(Proverbs 16:25)

ACKNOWLEDGMENTS

I offer a genuine statement of gratitude to all those who have kept me covered with fervent prayer and encouragement. I do not claim to be the idealistic version of a "man of God"—yet, God clearly gave me a directive and vision for writing this book.

Along the way, much spiritual warfare and personal feelings of inadequacy have become roadblocks to this mission. Your prayers and encouragement have been vital to the goal of bringing this book to publication.

In part, I wish to list some of those people so essential to the fruition of this work:

Carol Jean Blakely, Cliff Stogner, and Exodus Prison Ministry, for your diligence in processing the original manuscript of this book into the standard necessary for publication.

John B. Bryant, Pastor, Unity Baptist Church, Texarkana, Texas, for wise biblical counsel and for remaining a beacon of integrity.

Shawn Crane, Associate Pastor of Worship, Unity Baptist Church, for your media assistance with photos.

Jonathan Bryant, for the fantastic work you did on creating this book's front cover design . . . thank you.

Charles and Barbara Beard, for encouraging me to write a book; for your early influence of Christ-likeness in my life; and for keeping me mindful that God is in control.

Nathan Byers, Franklin Wilson, Benton Morrison, E. J. Turk, Myron Mosley, Michael 'Soldier' Denison, Phillip Rutledge, Faustino Ricoy, Tracey Davis, Tom Kewish, David Moore, Mike Estes, D'Andre Davis, Steven Wiley, David Almazan, Martin Zorilla and all my other accountability friends (I wish I could list you all), who have continuously reminded me in the midst of the battle to pick myself up and move forward in the Lord Jesus Christ.

Alvin and Janie Beaird, for reminding me of my potential in Christ, and encouraging me to hold my shoulders high in spite of the storm. My son could not be blessed with more loving and God-honoring maternal grandparents than the two of you.

Charles Gill, for your friendship and accountability. Your words have so often been an anchor which has kept me from drifting on more than one occasion.

Gary Raines, Chaplain, Texas Department of Criminal Justice (and your staff: Nick, Al, Greg, Grady), for opening your door to me and allowing me to exercise my gifts as a prison missions pastor-teacher, and worship-leader, for your leadership and reinforcement in bringing the gospel of Jesus Christ to the lost.

My parents, Herschel "D" Brown, Jr. (who is now present with the Lord) and Doris A. Brown, for raising my sister Teri, brother Rocky, and me in a loving Christian home. We love you so very much.

God (Father, Son, Holy Spirit), for allowing me to experience life, and (through your blood) to experience life eternal.

John Allen Brown
(Colossians 1:12-14)

CONTENTS

FOREWORD
by
Pastor John B. Bryant

Sexual addiction is not just a problem in this world; it is a problem with those who are citizens of another world. Within the church today, we find many strugglers —people who have sexual addictions or at least battle with impure thoughts. Many of these people are "masked" and will never be known. Most of them would never admit that they have such a problem, but it is there and it is real and for many, it goes unchallenged.

When an author begins writing a book, often you will find him in a mountain chalet or a lake house trying to get some inspiration from solitude. It might be that he has all the comforts around him to make it easier for him to meditate and contemplate. Yet, as John Allen Brown wrote this book you have before you, his inspiration was drawn from a life of sin, addiction, and years in prison. John never actually dreamed of growing up and going to prison. In fact, he grew up in a loving Christian family. I have had the opportunity of pastoring his parents and grandparents, as well as John. His mother, who is still living, is a dear, faithful, loving and sweet lady that I admire as a tower of strength.

The writing of John Allen Brown is from years of Bible study and invaluable life experience. John has a unique way of communicating the truth of the Word. His skills are incomparable and his experiences lend credence to his written words. To hear him speak is captivating.

His knowledge of the Word of God and his practical way of applying it will feed your soul.

Because of the downward spiral of John Allen Brown and his subsequent rescue from sexual addiction by the Lord, we have been given a gift. This gift comes to us in the form of words from life experience. The words in this book come from a man who has hit rock-bottom and has been lifted up by our gracious and merciful Savior, Jesus Christ.

Please read this book for yourself and your spiritual well-being. If you are not needing this book personally, I believe there is someone you know who does. Read it for them.

John B. Bryant
Senior Pastor
Unity Baptist Church
Texarkana, Texas

INTRODUCTION

What qualifies me to write a book about escaping the besetting sin of sexual addiction? Well, I am a man who has been delivered from the slavery to such an addiction. *Delivered* does not imply that I am now immune to sexual temptation; it simply means that, by God's active and operative Holy Spirit power in my life, I have a day-to-day victory over the power of sexual addiction.

For purposes of this book I would like to clarify the definition of sexual addiction as: *the persistent compulsive preoccupation with sexual gratification.* Although sexual addiction can manifest itself in multifarious ways from individual to individual, it always involves a persistent compulsive preoccupation with the gratification of whatever sexually immoral tendencies the individual battles.

The first half of this book begins by outlining some of my personal history concerning sexual addiction. This is followed by a chapter on the present and prevailing nature of sexual addiction in our world today, including the ever-increasing occurrence within the Church. Then some common questions the sexual addict often silently asks are dealt with, such as "Why am I this way?" and "Is there hope for me?"

The second half of this book provides four biblical applications which will serve as a "detonation switch" for the active and operative power of God's Holy Spirit to enable the sexual addict to resist compulsive sexual behavior.

As you begin reading this book, I want you to know I used no illusory padding of glamour to embellish my own personal history with sexual addiction. In fact, I expect there will be a number of people who reject *future* association with me after reading about my *past*.

Why, then, would I want to disclose such sensitive information in a book for all the globe to read? Actually, there is a simple explanation. Do you remember the biblical account recorded in *Mark 2:1-12* of four men who brought their paralyzed friend to Jesus for healing? The paralyzed man was lying on a mat as his friends got him to Christ. In *verse 11*, Jesus said to the man:

> *"Stand up, take your mat, and go on home, because you are healed!"* (NLT)

Notice that Jesus didn't just tell the man to stand and go home. Jesus also told the man to *"take your mat."* Why would Jesus tell the man to take that stinking, bedridden mat with him when the man no longer needed it? The man could now walk, jump, run, dance! He didn't need that mat! Couldn't he just drop it off at the nearest dump?

I'll tell you at least one of the reasons Jesus told that man to take his mat with him: *The man's mat was now his testimony!* Oh sure, it had the repulsive stench of bedsores and sickness all over it, but as the man walked home with that mat under one arm, and a big grin on his face, he could point to that mat and proclaim to the passersby that Jesus had healed him! Jesus had delivered him from his bondage of paralysis! I can imagine the man kept that old mat for the rest of his life and used it as a means of witnessing to the delivering power of Jesus Christ.

Likewise, my personal history with sexual addiction is my *mat*. I initially wanted to leave it behind and forget I had even been confined to such a thing as sexual addiction. My *mat* has a stench to it that a number of people will likely find repulsive; however, it is a part of my testimony and, through this book, I point to it and proclaim to the passersby that Jesus has delivered me from the bondage of spiritual paralysis that sexual addiction once had on my life! Praise God!

I also believe it is my obligation to speak out about the fact that the Lord has delivered me from the crushing slavery of such an addiction:

> ***"Has the LORD redeemed you? Then speak out! Tell others*** *he has saved you from your enemies."*
> (Psalm 107:2 [NLT])

May God bless you in a very special way as you read, re-read, study and put to practice the four applications outlined in the second part of this book. These will detonate the active and operative power of God's Holy Spirit in your life and alter the entire landscape of your soul for continuous day-to-day victory over sexually immoral behavior.

John Allen Brown
(2 Corinthians 5:17)

PART ONE

My Personal Story

"This is a true saying, and everyone
should believe it: Christ Jesus
came into the world to save sinners—
and I was the worst of them all. But that is why God
had mercy on me, so that
Christ Jesus could use me as a
prime example of his great patience
with even the worst sinners.
Then others will realize that they, too, can believe
in him and receive eternal life."

(1 Timothy 1:15,16 [NLT])

~ Chapter One ~
A Journey Forward

My earliest memories of sexual interest date back to kindergarten. One of my female classmates and I would play "doctor" during recess as we hid underneath the clapboard schoolhouse which was elevated off the ground a few feet by concrete blocks. Throughout the ensuing years of childhood I had an ongoing inquisitiveness about sexuality which may have surpassed the typical curiosity of a child; I often thought about and desired sexual contact long before I understood sexual gratification.

I grew up in a marvelous Christian family. There is truly not a thing about which I can express dissatisfaction—I was never molested by my family; there was no alcohol or drug abuse within my childhood home; I was never beaten, or any other external agents which so often wound a child spiritually, mentally, emotionally, and physically. In fact, the chief quality which best describes my childhood home is *love.*

Mom and Dad were faithful to the Bible, especially as it taught to:

> *"Train up a child in the way he should go..."*
> (Proverbs 22:6)

As a result, my younger sister, older brother and I were not only raised in a wonderful Christian family, but we were also blessed with the fabulous experience of church family. Being part of a church is a lot like having a hundred moms, dads, brothers, sisters, grandparents, aunts, uncles, cousins who all love you.

My first recollection of church fellowship goes back to the early 1970's when I was about eight years old. Liberty

Baptist Church was the name of that little red brick building with a steeple on top. I vividly remember the Sunday morning on which I made the decision to receive Jesus Christ as my Lord and Savior. The pastor had finished his sermon and stepped down from the pulpit to stand facing the congregation as the pianist played a hymn of invitation.

In the Baptist church we refer to this invitation as an altar call—as the congregation stands and softly sings the closing hymn, the pastor calls [invites] anyone to walk forward and receive Jesus as Lord and Savior.

Before that morning church service ever commenced, I had already decided I was going to walk forward at the altar call. I was strategically sitting at one end of the pew so all I had to do was step into the center aisle and walk forward to where the pastor was standing.

As the closing hymn played, I took that step and embarked on my journey forward. The pastor smiled as he observed me moving in his direction. As I met with the pastor in front of the congregation, I stated my desire to receive Jesus Christ as Lord and Savior. He asked me a few questions to determine if I understood what I was doing. We said a prayer together and he signaled for the pianist to end the hymn.

Standing there with my pastor, he announced my decision to follow Jesus. Several "amens!" were heard throughout the assembly, then a closing prayer was given.

Following that closing prayer, it was a tradition at Liberty Baptist Church for the congregation to come forward and shake hands with anyone who responded to the altar call. I was surrounded by hands and hugs of welcome into the body of Christ. There I was, eight years old, crying tears of joy as my heartstrings were flooded with such an awareness of pure love.

When a person receives Jesus Christ as Lord and Savior, a supernatural occurrence takes place within. In other words, the Holy Spirit of God unites with that person's spirit, and eternal life is given to the new believer as a child of God. (see *Romans 8:16; John 1:12; John 5:24*)

Along with the indwelling of God's Holy Spirit and eternal life, the new believer receives spiritual gifts—yes, even an eight year old child:

> *"Now there are different kinds of spiritual gifts, but it is the same Holy Spirit who is the source of them all. There are different kinds of service in the church, but it is the same Lord we are serving. There are different ways God works in our lives, but it is the same God who does the work through all of us.* ***A spiritual gift is given to each of us as a means*** *of helping the entire church."*
>
> (I Corinthians 12:4-7 [NLT])

"Each of us" who receives Jesus Christ as Lord and Savior immediately gets a spiritual gift(s) along with our salvation. Other spiritual gifts may be subsequently given to a Christian weeks, months or years following salvation; however, one thing is certain, if the Bible says that *each* Christian has a spiritual gift, that would mean the adult or child who became a Christian a split-second ago already has a spiritual gift as a result of receiving Jesus.

I did not understand this truth as an eight year old boy when I accepted Jesus Christ as Lord and Savior. In fact, as I suspect it is with most children who get saved, the spiritual gifts which God gave me were in germ form and needed to be cultivated toward maturity. For me, those germ form gifts included singing, preaching and teaching. However, as I said, I did not understand this truth when I received Jesus Christ as my Lord and Savior in 1974.

Following my reception of Jesus Christ, and the indwelling of God's Holy Spirit, I was baptized as a public profession of my faith in obedience to the Bible. It did not take long for my spiritual gifts to begin surfacing after my conversion experience. For instance, I began singing solos in front of the church congregation; I started carrying a pocket-size New Testament Bible to school with me so I could share the gospel with classmates; also, after Sunday morning services, I would go home to my bedroom, close the door and preach into a tape recorder as I attempted to emulate the pastor's sermon.

Just as I had been unacquainted with the doctrine of spiritual gifts, I was also oblivious to the serious nature of spiritual warfare which every Christian encounters as diabolical forces attempt to impede the development of our spiritual gifts, as well as our overall effectiveness as Christians (see *Ephesians 6:12*). Needless to say, we should thoroughly educate new Christians (whether child or adult) on the doctrines of spiritual gifts and spiritual warfare.

I am persuaded to believe that one of Satan's evil schemes is to deceive Christians into using their spiritual gifts in a worldly manner instead of for the glory of God and their church. In my life, the gift of singing for the Lord slowly started deviating toward a desire to sing for the world. The gifts of preaching and teaching (which would ultimately have required me to stand before crowds of people with a Bible in hand) started changing course toward an urge to be on stage and entertain. My evangelical tenacity incrementally de-escalated in scope and intensity as my fixation on fame and selfish ambition gradually increased. The shift in direction was almost imperceptible.

A couple of years following my salvation experience, I had enrolled in piano lessons, joined the school band and choir, and began studying dance at Carol Cooper School of Dance as a ten year old fourth grader.

You might be surprised to know what a kid can get away with in a fourth-grade language class. My teacher permitted us students to partner up and study together. One of my cute fellow scholars always let me slide my desk next to hers. We learned much more than the form and style of verbal expression outlined in our textbooks; our hands were busy studying *body language*...if you know what I mean.

By eleven years old, the closest thing to pornography I had seen was the womens' underwear section in those thick department store catalogues my mom received in the mail. I would sneak the catalogues into the bathroom, lock the door, and gawk at page after page of immodestly exposed women in their panties and bras.

Such images, without any question, were influential in how I looked at women. No matter what kind of clothing a female may have been wearing, I was beginning to learn the art of imagining what their panties and bra might look like underneath.

As a dance student, there were only two other male dancers at the Carol Cooper School of Dance. For whatever reason, those other two male dancers moved on to different interests and I was left as the only male dancer among all the females.

Whenever a dance arrangement required a male partner, I was the *one* who got to lift the girls into the air and spin them around. Lucky me—or so I thought. I was actually sinking into an even lower standard of immoral thinking because I was constantly surrounded by females wearing tight-fitting leotards and body stockings. Their immodestly-clad bodies (especially in my hands) were a cogent force toward sexual temptation and fantasy.

During the summer of 1977, a few months before my 12th birthday, I had some experiences which supplemented my impulses in the direction of sexual immorality. Our home was nestled in the piney woods of northeast Texas. The timberland beyond my backyard was a vast world of adventure for a young boy. With its tangle and trails, creeks and critters, I could disappear into the 1800's and become Davy Crockett or any other frontiersman my imagination could create.

During one of my trailblazing expeditions, I spied a hideaway deep in the woods where some of the neighborhood teens were gathered for drinking booze, smoking, and who-knows-what-else. When the teens left their little timberland haven, I went in to get a closer look. I found a partial bottle of whiskey and some pornographic magazines. I did not take a drink of whiskey that day, but it was my first time to see any totally nude pictures of women. I *drank in* every detail of every image on every page.

The second experience, during the summer of '77, which maximized my invitation toward sexual immorality involved my sixteen year old babysitter. The babysitter would often put on a bikini and sunbathe in our backyard. It was on a hot August day when my babysitter asked me if I would apply suntan lotion to her legs and back. I honestly do not believe she had any sexually immoral intentions in mind; however, it was an extremely provocative encounter for me. The feel of her skin in my hands added kindling to the flash of sexual preoccupation which had already been ignited within.

After I had turned twelve, a theatrical musical group toured through my hometown and performed at the community college auditorium. My parents purchased tickets and took my sister and me to see the show.

Subsequent to the program, there were auditions taking place in the lobby for anyone who might be interested in becoming a member of the tour group. One of the requirements for membership was that you had to be fifteen to twenty-one years of age. If selected, I would get to spend a summer of theatrical training at the American Musical Theater (AMT) in Petoskey, Michigan. Unfortunately, I fell short of the age requirement by three years, but I was not going to pass up an opportunity for theatrical training with the AMT.

My parents gave me permission to go ahead and audition. I informed the judge who would appraise my trial performance that I was only twelve years old, but would like to audition anyway. The judges gave me the go-ahead, but they made it clear that the AMT had never accepted anyone who did not meet the proper age requirement.

I began the audition by singing a song from the musical *Yankee Doodle Dandy*. I then followed through with a tap dance arrangement, and I finished up by playing a slow romantic song on piano. The judges appeared to be impressed; however, I was again reminded of the age requirement which stood in the way of my qualification.

I was certainly disappointed that I did not get accepted by the AMT, but somewhere down inside, I was hoping I would get another chance someday. That is when the unexpected happened. It was a few months following the audition when I received a package in the mail from the AMT. I tore into the parcel and could not believe what I read. There was a letter informing me that I had indeed been accepted for training by the American Musical Theater, beginning in June 1979, on campus at the North Central Michigan College. I would be assigned a dorm room for the summer.

Everyone was excited for me! Even the *Texarkana Gazette* came to my home, took pictures and interviewed me for an article. I felt sure that the AMT was going to be my first break into showbiz.

The day arrived for my pilgrimage to Michigan from Texas. My bags were packed as I gave farewell hugs and kisses to my family and boarded the massive airliner.

I had turned thirteen between the time of the audition and my actual departure to the AMT. I had no fear of flying alone, but there was a twinge of separation-anxiety from my family and friends as the airplane climbed into the sky and the world below became smaller.

We landed in Chicago where I connected with a smaller plane flying on to Michigan. By the time we touched down at Petoskey, I was ready to be on land again. Waiting for me at the airport was the Resident Advisor (RA) from the college dormitory where I would be living. She was a very nice young lady named Becky who would keep an eye on me and stay in close contact with my parents.

I was assigned to room # 222. It was evening time when I arrived at the dormitory.

"Where is everybody?" I asked. "The place seems deserted."

The RA informed me, "Everybody is attending a cast party going on in a cabin on the backside of the college campus."

I phoned my parents to let them know I had made it safely to my destination. Then I strolled over to the cabin where the cast party was in progress.

As I approached the cabin, I could hear loud music playing. The front door was standing wide open, so I walked on in. There was plenty of party food spread out on some tables, dozens of fifteen to twenty-one year olds having a good time, and beer.

Someone immediately offered me a drink from one of the kegs. I took it as if I was a knowledgeable thirteen year old connoisseur of brewed malt and hops. In reality it was my *first ever* alcoholic beverage. I liked the way it made me feel. It would be the first of *countless* more drinks of alcohol to come.

There is one thing you will not find backstage in theatrical arts—*modesty.* During a stage performance, many costume changes are done on the wings of the stage between scenes. There is certainly no latitude for hesitation when it comes to shedding clothing in front of other cast members—whether male or female. I got a regular eye-full of flesh.

There was also a lot of homosexual/bisexual activity among AMT cast members. One of the twenty-one year old men made a "move" on me while we were sitting backstage. I had never actually had any real sexual relations with anyone before, but I allowed him to do what he wanted—oral sex.

It was not long after that encounter that I was invited to watch some sexual interaction between a male and female who were both fifteen years old. I also managed to sneak my way into the female dormitory and spend the night with one of the girls. By the time I left the AMT at the end of summer, I had acquired great knowledge about properly inhaling a cigarette, drinking alcohol, and a wide range of sexual immorality.

Upon my return home to Texarkana, I remember sensing that things were not the same. Actually, it was *me* who was not the same.

My family was no longer members of the little church where I had received Jesus Christ as Lord and Savior. Instead, we were now attending First Baptist of Wake Village. It was a large church and very enjoyable. The youth pastor's name was Scott Neathery [at the writing of this book, he is senior pastor of the church]. Scott encouraged me to use my gifts for the Lord. I began singing again in church and experiencing a fresh spiritual momentum in my life. However, the summer of 1981 offered me another opportunity to return to the AMT in Michigan. It was a season filled with more alcohol and sexual immorality. I was now fifteen years old.

When I returned home to Texas after my second summer at the AMT, I started drifting from my dancing and piano lessons, although I maintained an interest in music by playing alto saxophone in the high school marching band and competing in the University Interscholastic League with my high school choir. My involvement in church activities began to wane at this time as well. Sin (especially a persistent compulsive preoccupation with sexual gratification) had gotten a foothold and set up a solid base of operation in my life. The deepest part of my being still knew that I belonged in church and that God had a plan for me if only I would not go astray. Unfortunately, astray I did go.

I began regularly smoking cigarettes and spending weekends with friends who enjoyed smoking marijuana, drinking booze, and having sex. I grew long hair and became a teenaged hoodlum. The Holy Spirit of God was constantly convicting me of my behavior. I never found any bona fide joy and fulfillment in alcohol, drugs, and sexual immorality.

I continued to grieve and quench the Holy Spirit as I traveled down a path which led me farther and farther away from God's will for my life, and further into the grip of sin's thralldom.

My behavior had become a deep concern to my parents as they decided it would be a good idea if I started seeing a Christian psychologist. I'm sure he was an outstanding doctor since his reputation was well noted in Christian circles. Nonetheless, I was less than honest with him about my alcohol and drug use, nor did I reveal the sexual activity with which I was involved. Following a brief series of counseling sessions, it was determined that my mental and behavioral characteristics were nothing more than some serious adolescent rebellion.

~ Chapter Two ~

On the Air

There was a small convenience store situated across the street from the high school. The owner had constructed a game room flanking the little market. The game room had all the current pinball machines and other amusement devices which could be challenged by inserting a quarter. There were also several dining booths where you could sit and eat nachos with extra melted cheese and savory toppings, or maybe a breakfast burrito or burger off the grill.

Every morning before school, and during lunch hours, that convenience store was a crowded gathering place for us high school students. As a sixteen year old sophomore, I had learned the art of spending idle time doing nothing with other high schoolers who were spending time doing nothing. It was while spending some of that idle time at the convenience store/game room that I first saw Keith Griffin.

I had noticed a yellow Camaro parked at the store for several mornings in a row. The fellow who was driving the car looked to be about twenty years old, definitely not a high school student. He would stand beside his Camaro with rock-n-roll music booming from his stereo system as a throng of people gathered around enjoying his company and having a good time.

"Who is that guy?" I asked one of my friends.

"That's Keith Griffin from Y-102 FM," responded my friend.

Wow! I had listened to Keith Griffin do his radio show from six to midnight many times on Y-102. My friend went on to explain that the reason he had been hanging around the convenience store lately was because he was dating one of our classmates.

Y-102 FM was the number-one rated radio station in town. Something about seeing Keith Griffin each morning at that store drew me toward the thought of becoming a disc jockey. *Maybe I could be as popular with everybody if I become a radio announcer*, I thought to myself.

In November of 1982 (the month of my seventeenth birthday), I skipped school and drove to the Y-102 radio studios around 10:00 a.m. I was greeted by a smiling receptionist as I entered the front office. I informed her that I was interested in filling out an application for employment. She reached into a desk drawer, retrieved the paperwork, attached it to a clipboard and had me sit in a nearby chair as I worked on the application.

When finished, I returned the application to the receptionist and she escorted me into a room where I was told to have a seat and wait a few minutes until the program director could speak with me.

As I sat waiting, it was obvious I was sitting in a broadcasting studio. The wall in front of me had a large soundproof plate glass window allowing a view into another broadcasting studio where a disc jockey was doing a radio show, Y102's "sister station" which was a country music AM signal. The wall behind me also had a plate glass window allowing a view into another broadcasting studio where a disc jockey was doing a show on the popular Y-102 FM. (I later learned that the studio in which I was sitting served as a newsroom for the journalist J. R. Carr).

I took a look at the control panel in front of me with all its knobs, switches, and meters. There were turntables and a reel-to-reel machine. The studio also contained a teletype printing device which had a continuous scroll of paper threaded through it for receiving news stories from *The Associated Press* as they were sent down the wire. The teletype machine was sitting silent when I had entered the room, so it startled me a bit as the device came to life and began typing out a story at rapid speed. Then it was silent once again.

After about five minutes of waiting, two men walked in and greeted me. They had my application in hand and introduced themselves. They really didn't need to introduce themselves because I recognized their voices as soon as they began speaking. The senior program director was Don Michaels, who also hosted the Y-102 morning show, and the assistant program director was Bob Stroud who hosted the Y-102 afternoon show.

They asked me a few questions, ripped a news story from the teletype and handed the story to me. They told me they were leaving the room but would return a few minutes later. I was instructed to push the recording button on the reel-to-reel machine and read the news story into the microphone when they left the room.

As soon as they left I recorded the story and pressed the stop button on the reel-to-reel. Don and Bob came back into the room, listened to the recording and said, "Not bad." I was asked to give them a few days to discuss it and I was informed that they would call me if they decided to hire me.

A week had passed since I filled out the application for Y-102. I was considering giving the radio station a call to see if maybe they had tried to get in touch with me. *Had I missed their call?* I wondered.

It was a little after 4:00 p.m. as I walked into the house following a day at school. The telephone was already ringing before I had gotten the door unlocked. I ran to answer the phone as quickly as I could, "Hello?"

"Yes, is this John Brown?" It was Bob Stroud's voice and I recognized it immediately.

"This is John Brown," I responded calmly.

"John, this is Bob Stroud from Y-102 FM, are you ready to come to work?"

"I'm ready, yes, anytime you'd like me to be there."

"Can you come in tomorrow afternoon as soon as you get out of school?"

"I'll be there around 4:00."

"We'll see you then, John."

"Yes sir, thank you very much, I'm looking forward to it," I said as I hung up the phone.

I tried not to sound overly excited as Bob was talking to me on the telephone. However, as soon as we hung up, I let out an ecstatic yell of exhilaration that might have vibrated the windows—in the neighbor's house. I couldn't believe it! I was going to work for Y-102 FM!

I could hardly wait to get out of school and report for my first day of work. I arrived at the radio station around 4:00 and was taken into the AM-station studio where I was introduced to the man who would be training me.

The AM station played country music and also served as a sports station as well. I learned how to turn on the microphone and give a legal station identification at the top of the hour. The only other task I was allowed to do was push buttons when it was time for commercials.

From the AM-studio I could see through the big plate glass window across the newsroon, and into the Y-102 FM studio where Bob Stroud was doing his afternoon show. Around 6:00 p.m., Bob was ending his program when I saw Keith Griffin walk into the FM-studio. I had never actually met Keith Griffin, but my goal was to become as good as he was, and hopefully as popular.

After a few weeks of training, I had learned how to properly spin records and talk on the air. I was mostly doing basic on-air work during the weekends for the AM-station, but I had also introduced myself to Keith Griffin and started spending time sitting in the Y-102 studio watching him do his nightly show. I was mesmerized by the magic of radio broadcasting. Keith was teaching me the methods which had made him shine above all other broadcasters in town.

Keith wasn't into drugs, but he highly enjoyed drinking alcohol, listening to loud music, and connecting with women. We became instant friends and party comrades.

One evening after I had known Keith a few months, I was sitting in the studio watching him do his show when he received an emergency phone call from home. He had to leave the studio right in the middle of his program.

"You want to finish my show for me?" Keith looked at me and asked.

"I can handle it," I said as the adrenaline began to flow through my veins.

Keith walked out the door and there I was, at the helm of the Y-102 FM studio. When the song came to an end, I put on Keith's headphones, turned on the microphone and said, "Y-102 FM, Stereo 102.5, Keith Griffin is out of here, John Brown is *on the air*!"

Following that night on Y-102 I began doing part-time work on the AM *and* FM stations. One thing I learned real fast was that the radio station request lines served as a link to countless females who wanted to "party".

Girls—young and old—called regularly wanting to meet with me after my radio show. I began having sex with different females every time I finished a radio shift. Along with the sexual promiscuity, my drinking and marijuana use became heavier as well. By the time my junior year of high school was completed in 1983, I had failed to pass into my senior year. Against the wishes of my parents, I became a high school drop-out. I earned my general equivalency diploma and began pursuing my career in radio broadcasting.

In 1984, I was finally hired full-time to host a midday show on Y-102 FM. It was a highly coveted position for an eighteen year old. Not long after I started my full-time gig with Y-102, I moved out of my childhood home and started splitting rent on a two-bedroom house with a fellow disc jockey.

We turned the house into a continuous den of sexual immorality. Group sex became a nightly norm as my roommate and I invited our radio listeners over to "party".

My sexual behavior had become a compulsive preoccupation with me, as was my drinking. I had reached a stage of addiction to sex, as well as alcoholism. My dependency on booze was so serious that I had to drink in the mornings, and throughout the day in order to function.

One day during my midday show I began having a need for alcohol. I put on an album and snuck out of the radio station unnoticed by the other employees. I got in my truck and drove to a liquor store where I purchased a bottle of whiskey, got back in my truck and sat there in the liquor store parking lot drinking whiskey, listening to Y-102 FM until the album came to an end and all that was on the radio was the needle scratching against the end of the record on the turntable. Someone at the station figured out I was gone and put on another song. Needless to say, I lost my job that day with Y-102.

The reality began to sink in concerning how stupid I had been by losing my job. A few days later I went across town and applied for employment at another radio station. I was hired and given a radio show on a country music FM-station.

It was only a short time until my drinking and reckless lifestyle caused me to lose that job too. This pattern continued as I went from one radio station to another, getting hired and getting fired. By 1988 I was a twenty-two year old washout in Texarkana radio and the surrounding area. My name was associated with the idea of: *He has great talent, but too bad he's a drunkard.*

My friend, Keith Griffin, had worked his way to major-market radio in Charlotte, North Carolina. He was now married and had two children. I gave him a phone call and told him I needed out of Texarkana. He told me I could come live with him and his wife in Charlotte, and he would help me get a radio job in that market. I wasted no time packing my bags and driving eighteen hours to North Carolina.

I became a member of Keith's family in Charlotte. When Keith and his wife Cheryl were working, I took care of their children. When Keith and Cheryl weren't working, he and I were out on the town drinking and basking in *his* popularity as a radio star.

Keith kept his word and got me a job working for a large radio/television broadcasting affiliate of *NBC*. It was a standard occurrence to have big-name celebrities walking the halls of the massive broadcasting complex. I felt I had finally "arrived" in my radio career since the morning show host was making a six-figure salary, and I determined I was just as good or better than he. Thus, I set my sights on becoming a morning show host in major market radio.

The problem I immediately ran into was the fact that I might have certainly left Texarkana behind, but I had not left *me* behind—my sexual immorality and drinking had continued to escalate with intensity. I was now using other drugs, as well, like intravenous methamphetamine, cocaine, lysergic acid diethylamide (LSD), and *any* pills I could get my hands on.

One night it almost all came to an end after a day of excessive indulgence with cocaine. I was sitting in a crowded nightclub and making frequent trips to the restroom between beers so I could snort another line of cocaine. My heart began to beat swiftly as if it were going to explode in my chest. I could not slow it down and knew I was about to drop dead right there inside that club as my breathing became difficult.

I didn't want to die in front of all those people so I rushed out of the building and walked behind the nightclub. I began praying that God would let me live. All I could think about was how shocked and saddened my mom and dad would be when they got news that I had been found dead from a drug overdose. *What would my sister think? What about my brother? What would all my loved ones and friends think and feel?*

"Oh, God, please let me live! I won't ever touch drugs again!" I pleaded with the Lord.

My heart gradually decelerated to a more normal rate. I left the club and didn't touch cocaine again for several years.

While in Charlotte, my persistent compulsive preoccupation with sexual perversion had plunged to deeper levels of degeneracy as I began using prostitution services and promiscuous sexual interactions with absolutely no regard or *any* moral boundaries.

The same employment pattern which had developed in Texarkana was starting to unfold in North Carolina as well—I went from one radio station to another, getting hired and getting fired. Although Keith and Cheryl expressed a deep regret in doing so, they asked me to leave their home because I had become someone they no longer knew. Since my car was in no condition for making a trip back to Texarkana, I purchased a bus ticket and left for Texas.

When I arrived home in Texarkana I moved back in with my mom and dad. I managed to get a job working for one of the radio stations with whom I had previously been employed.

Via the radio station request line, I started having regular conversations with a young girl who had recently given birth to a baby and placed the infant for adoption. One night I finally arranged to meet this girl face-to-face. She was fourteen years old and I was twenty-three. We established a sexual relationship and, with her parents' permission, she started living with me in a motorhome located in the backyard of my mom and dad's house.

Due to my alcoholism and drug abuse I lost my radio job. My girlfriend and I moved to a small town in Arkansas where I was able to secure a broadcasting position at yet *another* radio station. As my usual manner of behavior went, I also lost that job and we relocated to an apartment in Texarkana.

I got a job doing deejay work for a popular nightclub where my drinks (and the female bartenders) were free. One Friday night the club manager was attacked while confronting a few disorderly patrons. After the club closed at 2:00 a.m. I approached the manager with a suggestion. Since the nightclub had no "official" bouncers, I offered my services. I told him that I would continue working in the deejay booth, but for a little extra cash I would also handle any disorderly customers. I went as far as telling him that he could test my "skills" by having me fight two people of his choice on the dance floor before the club opened the following day. [Note: I had indeed won my share of fights, but thank God the manager did not call my bluff and have me fight two people *of his choice*; I would have been beaten to a pulp.] The manager hired me as his deejay/bouncer.

During my brief few months as a bouncer I was only called from the deejay booth three times: I had to escort a customer out of the club after he decided to urinate in the corner pocket of a pool table; I had to jump in the middle of a brawl in the vestibule of the club; and I used a canister of mace to motivate two men out of the building after they persisted in making unwelcome advances on a barmaid and threatening to come back and shoot me.

My real reason for becoming a bouncer wasn't the adrenaline rush or extra cash; rather, I wanted to make better friends with the manager so I could learn the code for the club's alarm system.

Each morning at 2 a.m. after the nightclub closed, I hung around with the manager until he would leave. I eventually learned the code to the alarm and planned my burglary.

One morning after the club closed, the manager and I were the last two people to leave. I waited an hour and returned about 3:30 a.m. I had secretly left a side door unlocked so I could get into the building without a forced entry.

I parked my car near the door and hoped no passersby on the boulevard would take note of my presence. Upon entering the nightclub I deactivated the alarm before it had time to be triggered by the breached doorway.

Instead of proceeding to the safe where all the cash was stored, I fast-forwarded straight to the bar. I then began putting as many bottles of booze as possible into heavy-duty trash bags I had brought with me. I never touched the thousands of dollars in legal tender stashed within the safe; but I stole every bottle of liquor I could get into my vehicle.

When I finished my illegal intent, I reset the alarm, locked the side door as I exited, then planted a forward thrust-kick into the door, bulldozing it open to give the appearance of a forcible entry. By the time the alarm sounded sixty seconds later, I was gone from the scene.

With my new acquisition of grog, I could now adequately drink myself into oblivion. I also drank myself out of a job at the nightclub, out of my apartment, and onto the streets.

My young girlfriend and I lived in our car until the vehicle broke down and was towed away to the impound. We then slept in parks, at the lake, and various places outdoors.

I was too ashamed of myself to go home to Mom and Dad because I didn't want them to see their son in such a warped condition. Nevertheless, God was *regularly* reminding me that He was waiting for me to turn back to His loving arms. For instance, I recall when my girlfriend and I were sleeping in a wooded area at the lake. We were both hungry and didn't have a penny to our names. The thought of catching a fish crossed my mind. I didn't have a fishing pole but I walked down to the edge of the water and began talking to God.

"Lord, I know I don't deserve any favors from you," I acknowledged. "I would just like to ask you to provide a fish I could share with my girlfriend."

That is when I spotted an old fishing line that was tangled in some brush and abandoned by a fisherman. I extricated the strand of line from the brush and discovered a small hook attached to the end. I then picked up a short stick and tied the line to the stick. Before making an effort to locate any bait, I gave the improvised fishing pole a cast to see how it felt. As soon as the *baitless* hook sank in the water, a fish swallowed it and took me by surprise. I quickly pulled the fish to shore and recognized it as a variety which is normally caught in deeper waters. As clearly as if God had audibly spoken, I knew beyond any doubt that He had *heard* and *answered* my prayer that day. I had just experienced His touch of grace and mercy, and I didn't feel quite as lost and alone; I was granted a measure of much needed hope.

I was able to convince one of the local radio stations to give me one more chance at employment. To bridle my alcoholism while doing my radio show, I carried a syringe full of methamphetamine to work with me and made periodic visits to the restroom where I would inject a dosage of the stimulant into my veins.

Meth made it possible for me to regulate my drinking quite well. My girlfriend's dad just happened to be a meth dealer and an invariable connection for my drug supply.

At one point I had been awake for several days and my arms were riddled with needle marks from continual intravenous meth injections. Suddenly, the left side of my body became numb. I told my girlfriend to call an ambulance because I believed I was having a stroke.

As the ambulance transported me to the hospital I told the paramedic about my drug use so they could give me an appropriate treatment. When I arrived at the emergency room I was connected to an electrocardiograph to determine the charges of electrical potential occurring in my heartbeat. I was then administered some fluids, via IV, and the doctor instructed me to stop using drugs, go home, eat a small meal and go to bed.

When I got back to my apartment, another girl who was living with my girlfriend and me had straightened up my bedroom while I was gone. She had placed a Bible on my pillows at the head of the bed. I didn't even know we had a Bible in the apartment, but when I saw that Bible laying on my pillows I experienced a moment of clarity that could not have been more comprehendible than if God had spoken aloud. The message was luminous in my heart as I felt God's love and His desire for me to return to Him where I belonged.

By the end of 1989 I was a twenty-four year old alcoholic, drug abuser, and sexual degenerate living with my fifteen year old girlfriend. I was once again unemployed and on the streets when my girlfriend decided she had been through enough suffering and unhappiness so she went back home to her parents.

I crashed into deep depression after my girlfriend left me. One phone call to my mom and dad was all it took for them to let me know I was welcome to come back home.

After moving back in with Mom and Dad I landed a job working for a video rental store. It wasn't radio, but it was a job. One employee benefit was the privilege of borrowing any movies I wanted to watch. Of course, I wanted to watch movies which were located in the "adults only" section of the store. I began watching as many X-rated pornographic films as possible until any trace of morality that may have been left inside my heart was consumed.

On April 1, 1990, I was introduced to an alcoholism recovery program by a friend who had been sober for a year. My first recovery meeting went well and I sensed a great deal of hope. For the first time in years I was able to accumulate some continuous sobriety, as well as drug-free living. I changed jobs and started working for a machine shop at a local paper mill and decided it was time to move out of Mom and Dad's house to a place of my own.

I rented an expensive duplex apartment, but the only furniture I had was a waterbed. Anytime one of my friends would drop by for a visit I would joke with them by pointing to a place in my empty living room and saying, "That's where my sofa is going to be, so have a seat right there."

I met a lady in the alcoholism program who had two years of sobriety. She lived in Oklahoma, but we had become acquainted with each other during a weekend camping retreat which involved a number of alcoholism recovery groups from different states. We had sex with each other and went our separate ways—she to Oklahoma, I to Texas.

A couple of months later, following eighty-nine days of continuous sobriety, I bought a bottle of whiskey and got soused. One bottle of whiskey led to more bottles of whiskey and I abandoned my waterbed-furnished apartment and job at the paper mill. I drove to Oklahoma and moved in with the lady I had met at the alcoholism camping retreat.

Within six months after moving to Oklahoma, my new girlfriend and I were married in February 1991. The wedding was performed by a Methodist minister in a Baptist church. One of my friends from Texarkana had driven to Oklahoma for the wedding. When the bride and I withdrew to our marriage bed on the evening of our espousal, we weren't alone. As a wedding gift to my new wife, I allowed my friend from Texarkana to sleep with her. Over the course of our marriage, the unprincipled behavior of extramarital activities continued.

I began working for a radio broadcasting company in the Oklahoma town where my wife and I were living. The company owned a country music FM station and a gospel music AM station. I hosted a morning show on the gospel station from 6-10 a.m., then I walked across the hall to the country music station and hosted a midday show from 10 a.m. till 2 p.m.

Each morning as I hosted the gospel music program, I listened to the songs and remembered the more innocent days of my childhood at Liberty Baptist Church. Oh how I longed to experience that sense of spiritual purity I had encountered as an eight year old boy giving my life to Jesus Christ. I found myself wanting to open a Bible and talk about God's Word over the radio. Of course, I couldn't do that because I hadn't read a Bible in a decade or more. I certainly didn't try and give the listener an impression that I was a pastor or preacher; nonetheless, listeners would call and say, "Pastor John, would you pray for me today?"

The conviction of God's Holy Spirit was piercing through the spiritual blindness and callous I had developed because of sin. I found myself sitting in that radio station on many an early morning shedding tears of grief as a result of God's Holy Spirit speaking to my heart. I knew what I was *supposed* to be doing with my life. I knew God had a calling on me. Yet, there was another voice speaking to me also. It was the voice of my addictions saying, "Have another drink! Have some more dope! Have some more sex!" I responded by pouring a little more whiskey into my cup of coffee as I played another gospel song over the morning radio airwaves of southeast Oklahoma.

By the middle of 1991 my drinking had gotten so severe that I quit my job and checked myself into a detox hospital. Following two weeks of detoxification and classes designed to educate me on alcoholism and drug abuse, it was decided that I should check myself into a 28-day inpatient center located in Ft. Smith, Arkansas.

My wife picked me up at the detox hospital and drove me to the inpatient treatment facility where I was assigned a bed for my stay. I attended classes on alcoholism recovery all day long, Monday through Friday. Then I attended recovery meetings each night.

After a couple of weeks, instead of completing the 28 days, I decided I was well enough to stay away from the booze, so I checked myself out and called my wife to come get me. My wife had rented an apartment and gotten a job in Ft. Smith while I was in treatment. We determined to stay and make Ft. Smith our home, so I began looking for employment. The radio stations would not hire me, but I did get a job working for a soft drink distributor. As soon as I received my first paycheck, I went to the liquor store and bought a bottle of whiskey.

My wife and I continued our debauched sexual practice of inviting others into our marriage bed; however, I was also secretly purchasing prostitutes and participating in other incautious sexual activities. Yet, I developed a deep resentment toward my wife because of *her* infidelity. It finally came to a head one evening when I went into a drunken rage and began demolishing our apartment while screaming endless profanities at my wife. There was no way I was going to be physically abusive to her, so I took it out on the items she most cherished. My boiling rampage came to an end after I back-fisted the glass casing of a large painting my wife had recently hung above our sofa. A lacerating shard of glass slashed a deep dime-sized chunk of flesh from the top of my right hand causing a deluge of blood to spray.

I walked out of the apartment, leaving a track of blood droplets all the way to the nearby payphone where I called the owner of the broadcasting company I had worked for in Oklahoma. Following a brief conversation, he expressed a willingness to re-hire me and even offered to drive to Ft. Smith and pick me up if I could stop drinking and start work immediately. I walked back to the apartment and informed my wife that I was going back to Oklahoma without her.

The following evening the radio station owner from Oklahoma arrived in Ft. Smith and had supper with my wife and me. He explained that he not only wanted to hire me as a morning show host for the FM station, but that he wanted me to serve as operations director for the entire broadcasting company. I couldn't believe the opportunity he was offering. I kissed my wife goodbye and was on my way back to Oklahoma. A few weeks later my wife left Ft. Smith and joined me in the Sooner state.

I was in no condition to handle the responsibilities of operations director for a broadcasting company. It didn't take long for the owner to figure out I was drinking heavier than ever. When he confronted me about it, I walked out of his office, drove home and told my wife to pack our things so we could leave town.

It was October 1991 when my wife and I left Oklahoma and drove to Shreveport, Louisiana. I had a friend there who worked in radio and allowed my wife and I to move in with him. I got a job working with KWKH radio, but my employment was especially brief because my drinking made it impossible for me to do anything else but drink. It was a this point that I decided I wanted to check myself into a detox hospital again for treatment. Benton State Hospital in Arkansas was willing to take me in without cost. I purchased a bus ticket, kissed my wife goodbye, and was on my way to Benton.

Following a 14-day stay in the detox hospital I returned to my hometown of Texarkana and checked myself into another 28-day inpatient treatment facility. I was issued a textbook the size of a New York City telephone directory and attended classes all day long with my elephantine manual which covered everything from A-to-Z about maintaining a *positive psychological attitude.* When I left the treatment facility after my 28 days were finished, the only thing I was positive about was the fact that I positively wanted a drink. Somehow I managed to abstain.

My wife had gone back to Oklahoma when I left her in Shreveport. When I finished my 28-day treatment in Texarkana, I moved back into my childhood home with Mom and Dad. I was 26 years old and ten years had passed since I filled out that application at Y-102 FM in 1982. My name had become synonymous with alcoholism in the Texarkana radio market. I was "blacklisted" in the radio industry.

I got a job waiting tables at a popular restaurant in town. After about a month I requested a job in the kitchen where I became a cook. Within about another month I was promoted to kitchen manager. I moved out of Mom and Dad's house and rented a home of my own. My wife came from Oklahoma to join me, and we continued the sexually immoral practice of defiling our marriage bed with group sex.

~ Chapter Three ~

A Catastrophic Crisis

Just as with most all of my jobs in the past, once my alcoholism became severe enough, getting a drink and staying drunk took precedence over anything or anyone else. My job in restaurant management was no exception. One morning I walked into the restaurant, realized I would rather go get drunk, so I walked right back out of the restaurant and drove to a liquor store.

It wasn't long until my wife and I were forced out of our house because we couldn't afford the rent. We moved in with a friend of ours we had met in the alcoholism recovery program. I needed to find another job as soon as possible because our friend had made it clear that we could only stay under his roof temporarily.

When I heard about a new radio station that had come to town I was determined to get a job working in the Texarkana broadcasting market once again. I made an appointment to meet with the program director and we talked about my radio experience. I filled out an application and he said I would receive a phone call if he decided to hire me.

After a couple of weeks of not hearing from the program director, I dropped in to talk with him again. He told me he had simply not made a decision about hiring me. "Do you want to have the number-one rated radio station in this market?" I asked him.

"Well, of course I do," he replied.

"Good, because if you don't want to be number-one then I don't want to work for you," I told him. "But if you want to be the top-rated station in Texarkana, I want to help you achieve that goal."

My comments seemed to work because I was hired on the spot before I left his office. It was 1993 and once again I had a job in the Texarkana radio market. A fresh start at a brand-new radio station was the ideal opportunity for me at twenty-seven years old.

My wife had gotten a job working for a florist. We were both employed but decided to go our separate ways and I got an apartment of my own.

It was refreshing to be part of a new radio station that was getting everyone's attention in town. Every time-slot, from the morning show to the overnight show, was filled with "top gun" talent (as we refer to major market quality broadcasters).

My time-slot was from 6 p.m. to midnight. I called myself "Wildman John Brown" on the airwaves, and a wild man I was. About thirty minutes before my show I would swallow a couple of pills referred to as "white crosses" (amphetamine tablets) so I could maintain my six hour high-energy level radio program and regulate my alcohol intake during the show. During commercial breaks, I would periodically go out to my car in the parking lot and take a few hits from a marijuana cigarette I kept in the ashtray.

From 6 p.m. to 9 p.m. I played lots of music and held radio contests to give away a bunch of free stuff. Then from 9 p.m. to midnight I hosted a popular request show called *Desperation Line.* By the time I finished my shift at midnight I had either arranged a sexual rendezvous with one of my listeners, or I would drive to a local nightclub and find someone to take home with me (even if it meant paying a prostitute fee).

Mr. T. (the actor from *A-Team* and *Rocky* fame) was in town as a spokesman for a national fighting competition. I first met him as he walked into the radio studio with two of his bodyguards. We shook hands and the interview began. We made sure the listeners knew about the upcoming fighting competition that was to take place at the fairgrounds arena.

On the night of the competition I was scheduled to broadcast my show from a ringside table. When I got to the arena the place was packed, and I was drunk. I sat down at the ringside table and began to broadcast. I can remember being so drunk that I was almost seeing double. Mr. T was at another table and politely walked over to shake my hand. After he had shaken my hand he walked back to his table. I decided I wanted to talk to him some more so I got up and began to stagger in his direction. His bodyguards immediately grabbed me and sat me back down in my chair. I was reeking of whiskey and very obviously intoxicated. My alcoholism was once again getting the best of me and it wasn't long after that incident at the arena that I quit my job *again* because I was too drunk to make it to work.

I eventually arranged a meeting with the management of the new radio station and practically begged to have my job back. The majority of management was against my returning, but the owner of the company agreed to give me another chance based on the recommendation of a radio consultant. *Wildman John Brown* was back on the air.

By the middle of July 1994, I had started attending alcohol recovery meetings again. I was still hosting the 6 p.m. to midnight show, but an opening for production director was scheduled to become available in August. I was interested in the promotion and applied for the position. I was granted the promotion to production director, but I also was required to change my time-slots and start hosting the midday show from 10 a.m. to 2.p.m.

At the time I was looking for a new apartment and was staying in a motel. My program director found out about it and insisted that I move into the guest bedroom of his and his wife's home until I found the right apartment. I moved into their guest bedroom on Thursday, September 1, 1994, just before Labor Day weekend. My program director and his wife had plans to go out of town for the weekend and I would have the house to myself. They left on Friday afternoon and were planning on returning Sunday evening.

Friday night was a quiet night for me as I cooked a steak on the patio grill and watched a movie before retiring to bed. I awoke early Saturday morning and drove to the radio station to meet a crew of people who would be accompanying me to do a remote broadcast for a few hours at a local business.

When I finished the remote broadcast I went back to my program director's home and relaxed for the remainder of the day. I had accumulated almost two months of sobriety and drug-free living. However, as Saturday evening set in, the thought of my program director's marijuana stash came to mind. I opened a small wooden box and rolled a joint. I smoked only part of the joint as I cooked another steak on the patio grill.

Sunday morning, September 4, I awoke around 11:30 and made a pot of coffee. I then showered and drove to the radio station to do some work in my office. By 3:00 Sunday afternoon I decided to take a break and drive to a nearby carwash. The day was warm and beautiful as I washed my car and thought about having a few beers. I drove to a store and purchased a case of beer and a bottle of wine. I then spent several hours driving around the backroads drinking booze and smoking the remainder of the joint I had rolled the day before. By sunset Sunday evening I was extremely intoxicated and stoned as I walked into a private nightclub and began drinking bourbon and cola.

The desire for sexual gratification became a preoccupation as I drank more bourbon. I got in my car and drove to an old drinking pal's home whom I knew had some daughters that might be interested in having sex. When I arrived at my friend's home around 11 p.m., he and I sat and talked in his front yard (actually he did the talking while I babbled with slurred speech). He informed me that he had stopped drinking and suggested that I not drive anywhere else until I sobered up. I asked him if he would be willing to get me a pack of cigarettes from a nearby convenience store as I handed him a five dollar bill.

As soon as he left for the store, I walked into his home and entered a bedroom where I had hoped to find one of his older daughters and talk her into having sex. Instead, a younger daughter was sleeping in the room. My obsession for sexual gratification was so great that I did not care about the girl being a minor, or her unwillingness to engage in sexual activity; rather, I grabbed her and forced her into my car and drove away.

An hour after driving on Interstate-30, my friend's daughter asked me to take her back home. Something in her voice made me realize the gravity of what I was doing. I turned my car around and took her back to her house. It must have been two or three in the morning when I let her out of my car at the entrance of a long gravel drive leading to her home. I knew the police had surely been notified by now and I half-expected cop cars to come out of nowhere encircling me with lights flashing and guns drawn . . . but nothing happened.

I drove to the radio station where I could be alone. There was no one else there because the station operated on an automated satellite system overnight on the weekends. I walked in the front door of the radio station and locked it behind me. Then I walked into the studio. I remember the lights were off in the control room and all I could see were the small, colorful lights on the control-board which gave the dark room a moonlit ambiance. It was sort of like sitting in a dark room that is illuminated only by the lights of a Christmas tree, or the small glow of final flames in a living room hearth. However, my state of mind came nowhere close to the peace and joy of Christmas and a living room fireplace.

I turned the speakers off in the studio so I could have total quietness as I sat in the broadcasting chair. I was wearing jeans, tee-shirt, and leather deck shoes without socks. I removed my shoes and leaned back in the chair while staring at the control-board. I began to process what I had done. *Did I really kidnap someone?* I thought to myself in unbelief. *I've crossed the line this time; there's no getting out of this one.* I knew that life as I had known it was about to come to an end. I got up and walked barefooted down a carpeted hallway and into my program director's office. I locked the door behind me, sat down in a chair and passed into a drunkard's sleep.

My eyes sluggishly opened around 6:30 a.m. I had heard something. *What was it?* I listened closely as my heart began to race with the sinking reality that this was not just a bad dream. The beastly morning after-effects of beer, wine, whiskey and marijuana had the inside of my head feeling like it was swarming with the static and atmospheric electricity which interfere with a radio or telecommunications frequency. My thinking was disbanded from any clear rationale.

I listened closely and heard some music coming from the studio control room up the hall. It was September 5, 1994, Labor Day Monday. Being a holiday, there was a part-time broadcaster hosting the morning show since all full-time employees had the day off.

Then I heard voices. Someone was talking to the disc jockey in the studio. *What were they saying?* I closed my eyes and listened harder. I heard them ask about the shoes on the studio floor. The disc jockey replied, "They look like John Brown's shoes."

"Who has a key to the offices here in the building?" one of the other voices asked the deejay.

`"I can call the program director," was the response.

"Yeah, call him, we think John Brown's in one of these offices. His car is out front."

I knew it was most probably a policeman who was asking the disc jockey all these questions. I knew there was no way out of the abyss I had dug for myself this time. The radio station breakroom was right across the hall from the office in which I was holed. For some insane reason I decided I would act as if everything was normal and just go to the breakroom so I could brew a pot of coffee. I lit a cigarette, unlocked the office door, walked across the hall. I began putting a few scoops of coffee into the filter when two police officers walked into the breakroom.

"Is your name John Brown?" one of them asked.

"Yes, it is," I answered.

"Mr. Brown, you are under arrest."

"Why am I being arrested?"

"You're under arrest for aggravated kidnapping and sexual assault. Please turn around and put your hands behind your back."

Handcuffs were put on my wrists as I was being mirandized. Barefooted, humiliated, and scared, I was placed in the backseat of a squad car and taken to the Bi-State Justice Building jail in downtown Texarkana.

I stood in front of the camera as it flashed. My mug shot was picked up by area television stations and newspapers. The story was a headline item.

The amount of time I was facing was 139 years in prison (20 years for state kidnapping charges, 20 years for federal kidnapping charges, and 99 years for sexual assault).

My clothing was taken from me and I was given a jail uniform which had previously been worn and washed so many times it smelled like a combination of body odor and institutional sanitizer. I was issued a thin plastic mat and a pair of rubber slippers for my bare feet. I was assigned to a small segregation cell which was bare of any decor; just hard, cold concrete and steel with a toilet and sink. I placed my mat on the floor, laid down and covered myself up with the blanket. I just wanted to hide from what was happening in my life. Plus, it seemed freezing cold in that place. *Don't they even adjust the air conditioning to a more comfortable temperature in here?* I kept wondering. The shock of my situation and what I had done to that girl was starting to sink in.

The chow cart rolled up outside my cell and a tray of food was passed through a slot in the door. A small polystyrene cup was filled with watered-down juice and handed to me as well. The jailhouse cuisine was far-removed from anything I was used to. I needed nourishment so I forced myself to eat it.

Tuesday morning I was awakened by the chow cart bringing breakfast and coffee. I quickly consumed the skimpy meal and began pacing back and forth in my small cell. I had a blanket draped around my shoulders in a effort to stay warm. My sleep had been less than restful. As I paced the gritty floor I started saying a prayer I had learned in my alcohol recovery program:

> "God, grant me the serenity to accept the things I cannot change; courage to change the things I can, and wisdom to know the difference."

I kept repeating that prayer again and again as I paced to and fro.

Nicotine withdrawal was beginning to get the best of me. *I think I'm about to go crazy! Why won't they let me smoke a [expletive] cigarette?!* I began to perceive that the walls in that little cell were closing in on me like a casket. *Only if I could just turn back the hands of time and make this all go away!*

Through a small window in the door, I noticed that one of the detectives who had been involved in my arrest was talking to someone at a nearby book-in desk. I knocked on the window and got the detective's attention. When he came to my cell door I asked if I could talk with him. He opened the door and led me to an interrogation room where we were joined by another detective.

"Can I please have a glass of water?" I had a severe case of cottonmouth.

Water was provided and I began trying to make excuses for what I had done: "I was in an alcoholic blackout and I thought the girl was somebody else."

Nothing about that explanation freed me from fault, blame, shame, or jail.

"You're going to do some prison time," one of the detectives assured me. "So just tell the truth."

I stuck with my rationalizations and disclosed as little detail as possible. Finally, I was offered a plea deal. The sexual assault charge would be dropped, the federal charge would not be pursued; all I had to do was sign for a 20-year sentence on aggravated kidnapping charges.

"I'll take it," was my answer. Twenty years sounded much better than 139 years. Eight days later I was sentenced to 20 years in the Texas Department of Criminal Justice—Institutional Division. I was immediately moved to general population (GP) within the city jail. My parents came to visit me and could not believe what they were hearing on the news.

"Did you really take a 20-year prison sentence?" they wanted to know. Mom and Dad were in total shock, not to mention public humiliation, about what was going on with their son. I attempted to ease their grief and distress by letting them know my court-appointed attorney told me I would serve no more than two years before making parole. The idea of two years in prison *still* seemed like an eternity at that point.

My cell in GP at the city jail had seven other men in it. There was a common dayroom area with television, and we all had individual rooms to sleep in—very small, with a bunk, toilet, sink, and writing table. One of my fellow inmates informed me that my attorney apparently did not know what he was talking about when I was told I would serve only two years on my sentence.

"Texas law requires all *aggravated* convictions to serve at least fifty percent of their sentence before being eligible for parole," he explained.

"What?!" I exclaimed. "*You* don't know what *you're* talking about!"

"Check it out for yourself," he replied. "You're going to have to serve at least ten years on a twenty year sentence for aggravated kidnapping."

I walked into my little room of confinement, closed the door behind me and stared out the fourth-floor window of the Bi-State Justice Building jail. If I could have jumped out that window at that very moment I would have done it. I had *never* felt more hopeless in my life. I wasn't just hopeless, but the idea of *ever* having hope somewhere down the road seemed irretrievable.

My routine reflex action toward any hint of emotional and mental unrest was always to "medicate": get drunk, do drugs, have sex; anything to render myself insensible to reality. Yet here I was, locked away from the drugs, alcohol, and sex. I couldn't even get a cigarette! *How am I going to deal with this overwhelming shame and turmoil in my heart and mind?!* I desperately cried from within.

I continued plunging into what seemed an unfathomable abyss of *peacelessness.* I stayed in my little room, isolated from the other inmates, and cried for hours at a time.

A correctional officer was passing out mail one evening and stopped at my door.

"John Brown?" the officer asked.

"Yes sir," I said.

"You've got a letter."

I took the envelope from the officer and he walked away. The correspondence was from a friend I knew in the alcoholism recovery program. Enclosed with a handwritten letter was a small page that had been torn from a Christian devotional book. There was a passage of Scripture at the top of the page:

> *"Be careful for nothing; but in everything by prayer and supplication with thanksgiving let your requests be made known unto God. And the peace of God, which passeth all understanding, shall keep your hearts and minds through Christ Jesus."*
>
> (Philippians 4:6,7)

Wow! I needed to hear that message from God! Now, listen to it in the New Living Translation:

> *"Don't worry about anything; instead, pray about everything. Tell God what you need, and thank him for all he has done. If you do this, you will experience God's peace, which is far more wonderful than the human mind can understand. His peace will guard your hearts and minds as you live in Christ Jesus."*
> (Philippians 4:6,7 [NLT])

I needed that kind of *peace* in my life—*"...God's peace, which is far more wonderful than the human mind can understand."* Those verses spoke to my heart as if God were communicating directly to me, and I guess He really was. I knew He was telling me to stop worrying and start praying. He wanted me to reestablish the intimate relationship we had begun when I walked down the aisle of Liberty Baptist Church as a little boy.

"Jailhouse Religion". That's what a lot of people in society claim happens to a criminal when he is faced with prison. I certainly won't dispute the fact that some inmates are double-dealing when they profess to have "found religion". However, the majority of "religious experiences" I've observed in the lives of inmates over the years are genuine in nature. The reason so many people who end up in jail turn to Jesus Christ is because incarceration is a catastrophic crisis which forces a person to face the inevitable insufficiency and futility of *self-reliance,* and the inescapable need for *God-reliance.*

This is not exclusive to people who find themselves in trouble with the law. Catastrophic crises come in many forms other than incarceration. For instance, the year following the terroristic attack in New York City on September 11, 2001, church attendance rose rapidly nationwide. Why? Because masses of Americans were able to see through the delusory sense of security we've built upon self-reliance, and they were able to recognize our ultimate need for God-reliance.

Catastrophic crises—whether terroristic attacks, terminal illness, prison, or any number of possibilities—have a tendency to bring people to the end of self-reliance, and face-to-face with their need for God-reliance.

With the door closed to my little room in the jail, I got down on my knees and started crying out to God. "Oh Lord, I'm sorry I've gotten so far away from you. Please, please, please, please, I need you. I need your touch..." I continued praying as tears flowed from the depths of my heart. "How could my life have come to such a place as this?" I thought about what I had done to that girl. "I'll live for you, Lord! I'll live for you from this day forward!"

Not too long following my conviction, I was transferred to the Bowie County Correctional Center across the street from the Bi-State Justice Building jail. The Texas penitentiary system was so overcrowded that I would have to wait in the county jail for almost a year before actually going to a prison unit.

The Bowie County Correctional Center was my first real taste of what prison might be like. I was assigned to A-hall, tank A-5. In A-5 there was about fifty bunk beds, one shower stall, three or four toilets and sinks, a television, and a couple of phones for making collect calls to family. A-5 was just a big cage for humans. Since all of the bunks were full when I arrived, I had to put my mat on the floor and hope I didn't get stepped on as I slept.

The room used as a chapel was directly across the hall from A-5 tank. When it was time for chapel services each week, I would make sure to attend.

Before long I was assigned a job working as a janitor inside the jail on A-hall. Part of my duties included cleaning the chapel. This allowed me plenty of time alone inside the chapel to just sit, think, pray, and cry.

As I got to know the chaplain he also allowed me to keep his office clean and do some light clerical jobs.

Working within the chaplaincy department really gave me a sense of fulfillment I hadn't felt in an extremely long time. As crazy as it sounds, there was a sense of eternal purpose in being a janitor/clerk for the chaplain.

~ Chapter Four ~

Razor Wire

One night in July, 1995, ten months following my arrest and conviction, I was loaded onto a prison bus with about forty other inmates en route to the Texas penitentiary system. As the bus made its way out of my hometown, I looked through the barred windows of that bus and wondered how long it would be before I made it back home. Ten years at the least before eligibility for parole. Even then, parole would not be guaranteed. *It could be twenty years before I get back home,* I lamented in my heart.

The bus ride was hot and cramped as I was cuffed to another convict who shared the seat with me. There was very little leg-room, and very little cushion on the seats. If we had to use the toilet—which was out in the open for everyone on the bus to see—the person I was handcuffed to was forced to join me (or vice-versa).

When we finally arrived at the intake unit in Tennessee Colony, Texas, I was ready to get off of that bus. However, as we drove through the back gates of the prison, I was struck with a great sense of fear. I had never seen so much razor wire in my life. Rows and rows of it inter-laced from top to bottom on the tall chain-link fenced perimeter of the prison. A broiling July sun caused the razor wire to shoot forth a blazing glisten that lacerated any measure of courage I was able to retain. *What have I gotten myself into? This is really happening? I'm going to prison!* The thoughts invaded my mind as I viewed the lofty gun-towers revealing correctional officers armed with assault rifles and (what appeared to me at the time) an urgent desire to discharge the high-powered ammunition at any prisoner who had even a thought of escape.

Any sense of pride, self-respect or dignity a prisoner might manage to possess is lost at the back gates of a prison. For example, the bus made its way through the gates and pulled up to a rear door at the intake building. We exited the bus, had our shackles removed, then we were commanded to get out of our clothes. There we were standing totally naked as officers inspected us for contraband which might have been concealed on our person.

Still naked, we were yelled at in a military fashion and ordered to keep our mouths shut as we walked into the building. We were then given boxer shorts and locked inside a chain-link cage, as cramped as a can of sardines, in the non-air conditioned building. The day-long process began: having my head shaved, showering with a chemical to kill any parasitic creatures I may have brought to prison with me, getting an inmate uniform, being interviewed by several staff members, having my mug shot taken for the prison identification card I would later be given, getting a number that would now become part of my name, eating my first penitentiary meal in the chow hall, getting a housing assignment, and (whew!) finally being able to lay down and try to relax after enduring the madness of it all.

The whole series of procedures involved with intake into the prison system has an extensively dehumanizing effect to it. The sense of one's individuality is progressively divested until he has the unmistakable awareness that he is merely an object which is known by a number while being warehoused away from society. Of course, prison is not intended to coddle the criminal. It is a forbidding place inhabited by people who have done forbidden things. I was now one of those inhabitants.

After my official assimilation as an inmate into the Texas Department of Criminal Justice (TDCJ), I was transferred to another facility called Buster Cole State Jail. It was now August of 1995, and the prison facility was just being opened. In fact, I was on one of the first bus loads of inmates to arrive.

The small complex was not actually an Institutional Division prison unit, but since the regular penitentiaries were so overcrowded, the TDCJ was sending a lot of us inmates to these State Jail Division units which were normally used for felons serving no more than a two year sentence.

I was assigned a job in the bakery. The four main edibles I was in charge of were: cornbread, biscuits, cake, and cookies. It wasn't a bad position to have. At least I could eat a lot, and I wasn't working in the "hoe squad" out in the fields.

The unit was so new that a chaplain had not yet been hired. The Sunday morning services were conducted by area volunteers from local churches. I attended as often as the chapel doors were opened.

A couple of months into my stay at Buster Cole, I was doing my bakery duties one morning when I noticed a man walking around in the kitchen area. He had on a nice pair of pants, a shirt and tie, but mostly I noticed the big smile he had on his face. He was shaking hands with the inmates (which was quite odd since you don't see much physical contact between staff members and inmates).

The man made his way over to the bakery and with that big luminous grin, he walked up to me with his hand extended and said, "Hello there, I'm Robert Huddleston, the new chaplain here on the unit."

"Good to meet you, my name is John Brown," I responded.

We talked a few minutes as he told me some of the plans he had for the chaplaincy department. I quickly asked him if he had hired a clerk. He said he had not, but would be doing so soon. I told him I would love to have that job, and I explained how I had done some clerical work for the chaplain when I was in the county jail. Chaplain Huddleston said he would be interested in interviewing me for the position and that I should fill out an I-60 (an official inmate request form) requesting an interview.

As soon as I got back to my housing area that day, I filled out a request form and dropped it into the unit mailbox. I was excited about the possibility of becoming the chaplain's clerk.

A few days later I received a "lay-in" (a slip of paper notifying inmates of scheduled appointments) which stated that I was due to report to the chaplain's office for an interview the following morning.

When I showed up for the interview, there was a line of about thirty other inmates waiting outside the chaplain's office. They *all* wanted to be the chaplain's clerk!

My turn came and I went into the office for an interview. I shared my testimony with the chaplain and, again emphasized the fact that I had done some clerical work and janitorial duties for the county jail chaplain in my hometown.

With thirty people vying for the job of chaplain's clerk, I knew it would have to be a "God-thing" if I was selected. Well, by the grace of God, the day following my interview, I was given notification that my job assignment had been changed from baker to chaplain's clerk. *Hallelujah!*

Chaplain Huddleston actually decided to hire two of the thirty applicants as clerks—myself and another man by the name of Mike Nunn. Mike and I became closer than brothers over the subsequent two years I would be there, and Chaplain Huddleston became our "spiritual father" as he took us under his wings and taught us a great deal.

Chaplain Robert Huddleston believed in allowing Christians "hands-on" experience when it came to active and personal participation in exercising spiritual gifts; thus, when I expressed my perception of God's calling on my life to the pastoral-teaching and preaching ministry, Chaplain Huddleston began giving me opportunities to teach and preach under his supervision. In fact, my first sermon was from the book of *Jonah* (quite apropos since the Texas prison system seemed to be the "*belly of a great fish*" for me.) When men walked forward and received Jesus Christ as their Lord and Savior following the sermon, I was hooked. There is simply no greater sense of purpose in this life than the eternal purpose of leading souls to Christ Jesus!

In June of 1997, almost two years after my arrival at the Buster Cole State Jail, an officer came to my bunk one night and told me to pack all my belongings because I was scheduled to catch a bus for transfer to another prison unit the next day. I was sad that my time with Chaplain Huddleston and the chapel congregation (my church family) had come to an end. *Where will the prison system send me now?* I knew I would be going to an Institutional Division unit—a real prison—and fear began to intrude upon my heart.

Again, I was handcuffed to another inmate and loaded onto a prison transport bus. This time I was heading to Huntsville, Texas. Huntsville is the hub for TDCJ. All inmates must funnel through Huntsville as part of the classification and unit assignment process. While there, I sat before a classification committee and was told that I was being assigned to the McConnell Unit in Beeville, Texas.

As soon as I walked out of the classification committee, I went back to the cellblock where I was being housed. Some of the older inmates ("convicts" as they prefer to be called because of their code of respect for each other and the staff) asked me where I was being assigned.

"The McConnell Unit in Beeville," I said.

"Oh, man! You're gonna die!" the convicts told me. "The McConnell Unit is the most violent prison in the system. It was just recently featured on a national news program."

I couldn't believe what I was hearing. Why God?! Why are you sending me to a place like that?!

The long bus ride to McConnell in south Texas was debilitating in the fiery July heat (prison transport buses do not have air conditioning. Neither do the prison units). I was thunderstruck by the massive size of McConnell and the enveloping perimeter of shiny razor wire. Almost three thousand felons lived within the labyrinthine confines of the maximum security prison, and I was about to join them—ready or not!

One of the verses that God gave to my heart in preparation for McConnell was Philippians 1:21:

"For to me to live is Christ, and to die is gain."

The Lord used that verse to bring peace into my soul by reminding me that I had surrendered my life to Him, and *wherever* I ended up, I was supposed to just keep living for Jesus. If He allowed me to die in the process then that was *"gain"* because I would be instantly in His heavenly presence:

> *"We are confident, I say, and willing rather to be absent from the body, and to be present with the Lord."*
>
> (2 Corinthians 5:8)

I got off of that bus at McConnell and walked in confidence of my Lord and Savior Jesus Christ.

I was assigned a cell on the second tier of E-wing. A maximum security prison tends to have an assortment of gang "families". The second day I was there someone approached me and offered "protection" if I was interested in hanging out with their white supremacy group. I thanked them for the offer but declined and explained that I'm a Christian and I'm hanging out with Jesus Christ. (I actually developed a courteous rapport with members from a variety of gangs during my years at McConnell. Some of them called me "John the Baptist". I had the privilege of observing several of these men lay down their "colors" and pick up their "cross" in full allegiance to Jesus Christ).

I was assigned to work the overnight shift as a trusty in the Administrative Segregation building. Ad-Seg, as it was referred to, houses some of the worst of the worst inmates in prison. Each Ad-Seg cellblock consists of single cells where inmates are locked up twenty-three hours a day, and only allowed out of their "lair" for an hour to exercise and shower.

The Ad-Seg building has a long central hallway running down the middle with six shorter hallways branching off by threes to the left and right. These shorter hallways lead to cellblocks. The last two cellblocks down the central hall housed the most incorrigible of the inmates supposedly incapable of being reformed.

Those last two cellblocks are the ones I most frequently worked on since my co-workers did not want to do so. I helped the correctional officers deliver breakfast trays to each cell (breakfast in prison is served between 3 a.m. and 5 a.m.). I would then help the officers go back around and collect the empty trays following breakfast. One morning an inmate had prepared a cup of liquid concoction consisting of urine and feces. When the correctional officer opened the tray-slot on the inmate's door to retrieve the breakfast tray, the inmate chunked the rancid excrement at the officer. The officer's reflexes were swift as he moved out of the line of fire. Unfortunately, I had been standing behind the correctional officer and did not see what was happening until it was too late and I was sprinkled with the mess.

The most disturbing duty I had in Ad-Seg was the task of cleaning up cells following an inmate suicide or attempted suicide. God illuminated something to me during a two week stretch when it seemed like I had to clean up a suicide cell almost every night. As I went into each cell to mop up the blood, I took a look around at the inmate's property in an effort to gain an idea of who this person was that lost hope to the point of killing himself. I noticed that in each of these cells there were Bibles. However, I also noticed that along with the Bibles there were other so-called "sacred" books—Koran, Book of Mormons, Jehovah's Witness New World Translation, etc…—and these men had been seeking the truth, yet they were trying to harmonize cultic writings with the inerrant and infallible Word of God. These cultic books were poisoning the men's souls to the point of self-destruction. It was like taking a glass of pure spring water and adding drops of snake venom before drinking it. God impressed upon my heart how severely lethal *false doctrine* can be to a person's soul.

1998. A year had passed since arriving at McConnell, and it had been four years since I had used alcohol or drugs. I was very active in the chaplaincy classes and programs which were available in the unit. However, I still *silently* struggled with sexual fantasies, desires, and habitual masturbation. My mental capacity for recalling all of the sexually immoral experiences from my past was fodder for stimulation. I would give in to the compulsions, and then I would experience an interval of guilt and remorse for my actions. I would repent and decree to never yield my mind to fantasizing and masturbation again. That decree usually lasted a week or two and then I once again became obsessed with indulging in sexually immoral gratification, give in, go through the whole guilt/remorse phase, then decree to never do it again.

Although my "cellie" knew I was a Christian, he started leaving his pornographic magazines lying around the cell. When he wasn't there I would take the magazines and place them under his mat so they would be out of my sight. The temptation to open them up and feed on the naked bodies was almost irresistible (considering I had not seen or touched the nude body of a female in four years). The thought of those magazines was constantly just below the surface of my mind. I could not stop entertaining the idea of seeing what kind of forbidden gratification I might find within the pornographic pages of those magazines.

It was only a matter of time when I finally placed a towel over the small window in my cell door so none of my Christian brothers would be able to see what I was doing. I opened the magazines and became consumed by the images my eyes devoured. Once again, I found myself in the sequence of guilt/remorse/repent/decree as I solemnly declared to abstain from any further sexual sin. Nevertheless, to no avail, I "secretly" and "shamefully" continued in the cycle throughout the years.

The head of our chaplaincy department at McConnell was Chaplain Lucio. He had a genuine heart of ministry for his captive congregation. One day Chaplain Lucio called me to his office. I had no idea why I was being summoned to see the chaplain. An order to report to the chaplain's office often meant bad news—such as a death or injury notification concerning family members.

When I walked into the chaplain's office he greeted me with a handshake and smile, then led me down a hall and into another room. I couldn't believe my eyes when I saw who was waiting to visit with me in that room!

"Chaplain Huddleston! What are you doing here?!" I exclaimed as we hugged.

"I'm down here in Beeville for some training so I thought I would drop in and check on you," he explained.

We visited for an hour or so and he asked me if I was doing any Bible teaching. I told him I was not doing any teaching, but that I was studying a lot and looked forward to teaching again. Before he left, he put in a good word for me with Chaplain Lucio concerning my ministry gifts.

Chaplain Lucio had an "inmate ministry team" which consisted of seven inmates who had answered God's call to ministry. This ministry team taught weekly Bible studies to an assembly of inmates on a regular basis, and occasionally preached other services as well.

I expressed a desire to become part of the inmate ministry team. Chaplain Lucio interviewed me to get a feel of where I was doctrinally and, with Chaplain Huddleston's recommendation, welcomed me to his team. I was about to embark upon a journey of practical experience that would become an invaluable foundation for the prison ministry to which God was calling me.

Fast-forward... The year 2004 was finally rolling around on the calendar. I had been on McConnell for seven years of the ten years since my incarceration began on that

Labor Day Monday back in 1994. Lots of things had happened over the years: My dad went home to be with the Lord; my wife officially divorced me; I had seen much violence, including the death of a correctional officer moments after he was stabbed by an inmate; I had gone through the massive changes which took place inside prisons when the "Texas Seven" escaped from a unit just thirty minutes from McConnell; a terrorist attack had taken place on American soil; technology had increased by leaps and bounds; mostly, I had changed into a much different man than the one who was arrested a decade earlier.

God had brought me a great distance, spiritually speaking. He had given me a clear vision for a jail, prison and radio ministry. He would have me start Shepherd Heart Ministries. He made it especially clear to me that I was *not* supposed to re-enter the secular radio broadcasting industry again. Those days were over; instead, I was to use my broadcasting experience for preaching and teaching the Bible on the airwaves.

My parole interview took place around September of 2004. By God's grace and mercy, through the prayers and support of my precious mom and her church, my parole was granted. I was transported to Huntsville and walked out of prison on the cold, sleety morning of Thursday, December 16. Praise God! I was finally leaving the *"belly of the great fish!"* I was finally going home. The song "I'll Be Home for Christmas" had a uniquely personal meaning to it as I boarded a bus (*not* a prison bus, thank God!) bound for northeast Texas.

I hardly recognized my hometown as the bus entered the city limits of Texarkana. When we pulled into the terminal at dusk, I exited the bus and looked through a plate glass wall into the waiting area. There they were! My mom and my sister Teri! I went on in and they spotted me. We were all smiling bigger than we had in ten long years. Oh, we had done plenty of smiling and hugging inside the confines of prison visitation rooms over the years, but the hugs and smiles were always interwoven with the grievous inevitability that we would shortly say our goodbyes and I would stay behind as they went home without me. Now, as we smiled and hugged in the bus terminal, the joy couldn't have been greater. No more goodbyes! We got in the car and went home.

As I write this, I just don't know how to describe the surreality of what I experienced when walking through the door of my childhood home after a ten year absence. The fact that my dad was no longer there is the first thing which impacted me as I looked around and saw his picture on a shelf. I sat down at the kitchen table and simply allowed the special milieu of home to enfold and embrace me with its smells, memories, and warmth. Somewhat blissfully disoriented, I desired to *never* leave the sanctum of those comforting walls again, lest I awake to find I was hallucinating and it was all a fantastic dream.

Over the first several days of being home, I was surrounded by kindred: aunts, uncles, cousins, a brother-in-law and nieces I had never met, my sister and brother, another niece I had only cradled as an infant in my arms a decade earlier, and a few friends. After so many years of sensory deprivation which comes from living in a "cage", I was absorbing every measure of the encompassing love of family and friends as a wilted flower would desperately guzzle the refreshing water being poured into its droughty and sun-baked soil.

Of all the people most elated to have me home was my mom. Here I was, a 39 year old man living with my mom; yet, there was no shame on my part or hers. It was so wonderful to wake up and enjoy breakfast with her at that dining room table which held so many memories of family meals from years gone by. She and I spent hours talking and taking trips into town together. Mom had been the one person to faithfully write me letters week after week during my years of incarceration. She and Dad were the only ones to remain constant in traveling the long miles to spend time with me in the prison visitation rooms. Now all of that was finally behind us and I was home.

The first Sunday following my release was December 19, 2004. I accompanied my mom to services at Unity Baptist Church. Although I had previously been corresponding with Pastor John B. Bryant via mail while I was in prison, I finally had an opportunity to meet him. Distinguished and outstanding as a Bible teacher, preacher and pastor, Bro. John was an example of consistent integrity and God-honoring purpose that I needed in my life.

Bro. John and I sat down in his study to pray about and discuss the ideas I had for Shepherd Heart Ministries. He recommended that I write a proposal of the ministry and present it during an upcoming business meeting at the church. The business meeting went well and Shepherd Heart Ministries was officially established as a prison outreach ministry of Unity Baptist Church (UBC). I started preaching in local jails.

On Sunday, January 9, 2005, twenty-four days following my release from prison, I had been invited by Bro. John to preach the morning service at UBC. I stood before an auditorium full of people and preached a sermon about "Christian Commitment". The message was certainly a powerful dispatch which God had placed upon my heart to deliver from the pulpit. However, even as I stood behind that sacred desk from where I was so privileged to stand, there was already a root of incongruity beginning to entrench itself within my own life as a messenger of such a message. As I preached about *commitment,* a contradiction to that charge as a Christian was dawning in the form of sinful sexual *compromise* within my heart.

I had made a compact with God, before my release from incarceration, agreeing that I would not become romantically involved with anyone for at least one year after arriving home from prison. God had impressed this upon my heart so I could have at least a year to establish a solid foundation and build the ministry in which He had called me to serve. I had no idea my compact with God would be so strongly challenged as soon as I was home from prison.

To abridge a rather detailed account, I will simply say that my re-acquaintance with an extraordinary childhood friend, who was enduring a difficult marriage, progressed into an adulterous affair within a few short weeks of my release from prison. We had once wanted to spend our lives together so many years ago, but our paths had taken different directions. Wasn't our reunion now a divine-appointment by God allowing us to finally be together and correct the wrong choices that had kept us apart all those years? We rationalized this question in our hearts.

Some obvious indications that our adulterous reunion was *not* a *divine-appointment* by God would be: The Bible's clear teaching about adultery; the heartbroken suffering, sorrow, and grief of her husband; the ruptured sense of security and home of their two young sons; the disgrace and discredit my actions brought upon me and the ministry to which God had called me; the grieving and quenching of the Holy Spirit in my life and ministry…(do I need to list more?) Sin is sin is sin! We can rationalize it all day long, but sin is sin is sin! Yes, it is paradoxically true that God's sovereign plan can still be birthed from amid even our most sinful of choices; yet, we should never find reason to rationalize sin:

> *"... you may be sure that your sin will find you out."*
>
> (Numbers 32:23 [NLT])

In the brevity of three months, my sinful choices had led me so far off-course spiritually that all I wanted to do was "run". I was no longer drinking booze or doing drugs as I had been ten years earlier, but the same pattern of "running away" when my life started falling apart, was no different than it had been a decade before.

I made a phone call to an old friend who owns several radio stations. He was glad to hear that I was home from prison and finally sober. He just happened to have a country music radio station in Sulphur Springs, Texas that needed a morning show host. I quickly accepted the job and transferred my parole to Sulphur Springs (an hour and a half toward Dallas from Texarkana). I signed back on the radio airwaves the morning of April 1, 2005.

The broadcasting company set me up in a duplex apartment and paid my rent and utilities. My morning show was a success with the listening audience and advertisers. I was soon asked by the broadcasting company's president to take over programming duties of four other radio stations while maintaining my morning show responsibilities. I could not believe how rapidly I was advancing in the industry after being gone for so many years!

On top of hosting and producing my own morning radio show, I was driving to Paris, Texas, several times a week to meet with the on-air personalities of the four stations I programmed there. The overall work load was intense. The task was not impossible, but it was consuming.

I had stopped attending church and ministering in the jails. I had essentially isolated myself from any form of solid spiritual support (although I still attended alcohol recovery meetings). My job became my life 24/7.

I did not regress back to drinking and drugs; however, my addictive behavior regarding sexual immorality began to manifest itself in the form of Internet pornography. I would sit for hours upon hours viewing the endless corridors of sexual darkness to be voyaged with the click of a mouse. It was my little secret. It was my place of escape where I could go and find forbidden release.

Although I never went back to using alcohol and drugs, I had no idea that Internet porn addiction is an addiction to another form of "drug". In fact, we might accurately refer to pornography addiction as an addiction to a "neuro-cocktail". Please be patient with me as I try to explain. The brain has a region called the frontal lobe in which a person's rational thinking is conducted. It is in this frontal lobe of our brain where sensible reasoning is used to determine benefits versus hazards of the various stimuli which bring us pleasure. For instance, I find immense pleasure in brewing a strong cup of coffee, opening an extra-large package of triple-stuffed cream filled cookies and dunking them one at a time into my coffee until I have eaten the entire package. I find such tremendous delight in this form of self-indulgence that I could easily do it every single day! However, the frontal lobe region of my brain alerts me, through intelligent rationale, to the unhealthy hazards of this behavior which outweigh the healthy benefits; thus, I choose not to give in to such conduct on a regular basis.

Underneath the portion of our brain which contains the frontal lobe is a region called the limbic system. This area is not governed by the conscious, rational mind. Our limbic system is subconscious and designed to serve as the brain's pleasure and reward transmitting site. Pleasurable stimuli cause the limbic system to react by releasing neurochemicals which create a feeling of euphoria. Some of these God-designed chemicals include endorphins (i.e., opiate-like compounds), dopamine, norepiniphrine, oxytocin, and vasopressin.

Each of these neurochemicals play a vital and specific role when combined within the context of God-honoring sexual intimacy between husband and wife. In fact, God brilliantly and artistically formulated oxytocin and vasopressin to serve as an emotional adhesive for developing and strengthening the ongoing oneness between husband and wife in the bonding process of becoming "one flesh". Together, these and other neurochemicals harmoniously blend into a "neuro-cocktail" which enriches and deepens the gratification and genuine fulfillment of biblical sexuality within the intimate retreat of the marriage bed.

It is only in the realm of sexual immorality that this "neuro-cocktail" works *against* an individual. The more a person ignores the intelligent rationale from his frontal lobe, warning of the hazards with sexual immorality, the greater the subconscious can influence behavior. This is what happens with Internet pornography addiction. The visual stimulus of pornography created an immediate release of the "neuro-cocktail" within my brain (especially when accompanied by masturbation). The problem is that porn, and any form of sexual immorality, is in extreme conflict with God's definition of healthy sexuality. At the core of our being (particularly for the Christian who is acting out in sexual sin), sexual immorality engenders feelings of shame, insecurity, restlessness, depression, guilt, remorse. Ultimately a deep sense of emptiness is experienced by the porn addict because the oxytocin and vasopressin which are being released in the "neuro-cocktail" are developing and strengthening his ongoing oneness and bonding process with . . . a computer! An image on a computer monitor can never take the place of true sexual gratification and genuine fulfillment found within God's design for healthy sexual intimacy. When a Christian enters into immoral sexual behavior, it may bring momentary euphoria, but it inevitably causes spiritual, emotional and psychological pain as a result of one's ruptured and broken fellowship with God. In order to deal with my own pain, I sought out more pornography in order to achieve another rush of "neuro-cocktail". An increasing flood of euphoria would ensue and I would experience an intense feeling of well-being. However, that feeling would soon get wiped out by the violent eruption of more spiritual, emotional and psychological pain caused by the misapplication of my God-given sexuality.

When the limbic system is abused, the snare of addiction is firmly secured because the brain actually begins decreasing the measure of neurochemicals which create euphoria. As a result, the sexual behavior which previously brought pleasure is no longer adequate to satisfy the yearning for a dosage of "neuro-cocktail". This is referred to as the *law of diminishing returns.* In other words, the visual stimulus of pornography began to diminish in its return of sexual gratification; thus, my persistent compulsive preoccupation escalated toward the hardest-core and outermost taboo websites as a means of trying to reach a heightened sense of gratification. My rational thinking about healthy sexuality had been overtaken by a drive to experience another round of "neuro-cocktail", no matter how perverted I had to get. Needless to say, pornography is not an innocuous pastime to play around with. Danger! Danger! Danger!

I didn't understand, at the time, any concept of "neuro-cocktails", and the law of diminishing returns; although, looking back, I can now understand how these factors play a big role in porn addiction. In fact, for the Internet porn addict, this *law of diminishing returns* is time and again the catalyst which precipitates the addict into an irrepressible urge to go beyond simply viewing porn, and physically acting out the pornographic activity itself.

Saturday, 24 September, 2005. Hurricane Rita was imposing a savage blow to the Gulf coast of Texas. Hurricane Katrina had tried to annihilate New Orleans from the planet a month earlier, and many of the residents from Louisiana had found refuge in Texas, only to be faced with the threat of another violent storm in the Lone Star State.

Rita hurled her cyclonic storm bands all the way to northeast Texas: bullets of hail; pummeling wind speeds; horizontal squalls of rain. I was at the radio station monitoring radar information and interrupting regular programming with updated storm reports for the local and surrounding areas. During the downtime between updates, I was visiting pornographic websites.

I should have taken a cue from Hurricane Rita about the "storm" I was about to invite upon my life with the click of a mouse. A website appeared on the computer's display screen. With a simple glance I could see that the nude females were younger than eighteen years old. Nevertheless, I clicked the palm-size device in my right hand and accessed the website. The next thing I know, a barrage of *illegal* sites began to rapidly appear on the screen. I shut the computer off and walked away.

My heart was pounding with a sense of both fear and energized eroticism. I stepped outside the front door of the radio station and stood smoking a cigarette. The wind and rain from Hurricane Rita was unyielding as I took shelter beneath an exterior appendage to the building. I could not get the forbidden images out of my mind. I finally decided that I was going back for a second look.

I sat down in front of the computer and turned it on. Then I began trying to get back to the illegal porn sites. *Where are they? I can't find them?* I went to the computer's "history screen" but could not retrace my tracks.

I went outside to smoke another cigarette. Would you believe I had the shameless boldness to begin praying? Actually, praying would have been a wise thing to do had it been prayers of *repentance*. Instead, I was praying for God's help in finding those prohibited porn sites!

"Lord, you created the female body; I just want to admire your creative work. I'm a man, and you hardwired me to want to look at feminine beauty. Please, help me find those websites again.

In Jesus' name, Amen."

I can't believe that God did not swiftly launch an angry flash of lightning out of the tempestuous firmament and zap me to smithereens for praying such a thing! I thumped the remainder of my cigarette into the air and watched the bright orange ember disappear as it was doused by rain and landed on the swamped ground. As quickly as the cigarette splashed down, it was dragged away by the swift and prevailing current of miry water streaming through the radio station yard. I should have taken a cue from that cigarette and realized that the 'ember of light' which was left in my life as an ambassador for Christ was about to be extinguished as I chose to plunge myself into a deeper deluge of sin that would swiftly drag me away by prevailing and miry currents of circumstance which I would regret for the remainder of my life.

I went back inside the radio station and sat down in front of the computer. Within minutes, I was able to locate the illicit websites. It was as if God had answered my prayers!

[Note: I do not believe for a second that God dismissed or honored my sinful actions by answering that prayer. However, I do believe that it is highly conceivable that God removed His hand and allowed me to access the websites so I could experience the consequences as a form of chastisement. (see *Hebrews 12:4-11*)]

I am not going to describe the things I saw on those illegal pornographic websites, lest I introduce the optical counterpart into your mind. All I will say is that I had never seen anything so sexually "hard-core" in my life. In my reprobate state of mind, some of the images were extremely sexually arousing while some were extremely repelling. I would be less than honest if I tell you I was not wanting to see more of the images those sites had to offer; nevertheless, I also sensed a potent demonic proximity in relation to those websites. In fact, one of the sites had an opening page which read: *"Welcome to the World of Darkness!"* I could spiritually discern that I had passed beyond a diabolical portal through which I was opening myself up to some profoundly destructive forces.

Suddenly a large red icon appeared on the screen. The icon indicated a virus had been released into the computer. My intent abruptly shifted from looking at porn to trying to figure out how to remove the virus. The more I endeavored to get rid of the virus, the more those red icons appeared on the display screen! I finally just gave up and turned off the entire computer. As Hurricane Rita died down, I left the radio station and went home, but the real "storm" was just about to kick off in my life.

I awoke around 9:00 Sunday morning and went to the radio station in hopes that *somehow* the computer virus had disappeared. I turned on the computer. The virus was still there.

Something had to be done to fix the computer before business started the following Monday morning. I got on the phone and contacted the radio station's computer technician. I explained that I had just come to the station and discovered a virus on the computer. I told him that I had no idea how it got there but he had better come take a look.

The computer tech drove to the station and took a look at the problem. He said it was impossible for him to figure out what caused the virus but he would take the computer back to his house and run a diagnostic to find the answer.

By Monday morning, 26 September 2005, business had resumed as usual at the radio station, but word was getting around the station that the computer tech had discovered illegal pornographic websites (i.e. child porn) as the source of the computer virus. By Monday afternoon, local police detectives were notified.

Tuesday, 27 September 2005, radio station employees were being scheduled for questioning at the police department. I was due to be interrogated during the afternoon hours. As I sat in that little room at the police department while two detectives quizzed me concerning my knowledge of the porn sites, I denied any involvement. The detectives brought up the subject of my felony record and years in prison, claiming I was the most likely "culprit". I continued to disclaim any involvement in accessing those porn sites, and I even offered to submit myself to a polygraph exam. The detective agreed to schedule the polygraph and I left the police station.

I was scared. There was no doubt in my mind that it was only a matter of time before the detectives put all the pieces together and arrested me. I knew I could certainly not pass a polygraph exam.

I drove from Sulphur Springs to Texarkana and sat down with my mom on Tuesday night so I could tell her what was going on. I admitted my guilt concerning the porn and informed her of my decision to turn myself in the following morning. My mom was especially devastated by what I was telling her. The implication was clear: *I would be arrested and sent back to prison!*

I stayed the night at Mom's house, but did not sleep too soundly. When I awoke at 3 a.m., Mom was already awake and had a cup of coffee ready for me to drink on my drive back to Sulphur Springs. I had to be on the radio by 6 a.m., so I gave Mom a hug and kiss and got into my vehicle. As I backed out of the driveway, the headlights illuminated my mom as she stood there waving goodbye. *Goodbye*…here we were saying goodbye once again. I took in the image of my precious mom and my childhood home as I knew it could be years before I ever made it back.

I did my morning show in Sulphur Springs from 6 to 10 a.m. It was Wednesday, 28 September 2005. I left the radio station and drove to the police department where I admitted to accessing the illegal Internet porn. I was promptly arrested and transferred to the county jail, once again wearing jail clothes and on my way back to prison. Back to the razor wire.

From the day I had walked out of prison in December 2004, to the day I went back in September 2005, nine months of freedom was all I experienced, but could I really call it "freedom"? I had made many bad choices during those nine months which contributed to my return to prison. Howbeit, one of the biggest miscalculations I made was to believe that as long as I did not drink alcohol or do drugs, I would not fall back into corrupt sexual compulsions. I had never seriously considered the fact that my problem with sexual immorality was actually an *addiction* in and of itself—independent from my former problem with alcohol and drugs.

I could continue writing and telling you about how much more traumatizing it was for me emotionally and psychologically to go back to prison the second time than it was the first time I was incarcerated in 1994. I could expand on the descriptive details of what I experienced as a result of going back to prison and the attendant consequences I have had to face because of my crime—perhaps I will save all of that for another time. You see, this book is really not about me. Oh sure, I certainly wanted to share with you the information communicated about myself in the first four chapters so you can see how far down the scale I had gone into the muddy and miry pit of sexual sin. Without any question, I wanted to reveal to you the fact that it took going back to prison before I could get transparently honest with myself, God, and other people concerning my deepest sexual frailties and weaknesses in order to find genuine recovery and restoration in this area of my life; however, as I asserted, this book is really not about me.

This book you are reading is ultimately about a Savior named Jesus the Messiah! By the power of His indwelling Holy Spirit—and my willing cooperation—Christ has lifted me out of the enveloping sludge of sexually immoral thinking and behavior. He has renewed my soundness of mind and has given me the firm footing I need for walking a daily life of victory over sexual impurity:

> *"He lifted me out of the pit of despair, out of the mud and the mire. He set my feet on solid ground and steadied me as I walked along. He has given me a new song to sing, a hymn of praise to our God. Many will see what he has done and be astounded. They will put their trust in the LORD."*
>
> (Psalm 40:2,3 [NLT])

This book is about what the power of our Living Lord and Savior Jesus Christ can truly accomplish in the life of a human being like myself. Listen, if He can deliver me, He can deliver you...no matter how far you have plunged into the darkness of sexual transgression.

Perhaps your sexually immoral battles come nowhere near the measure of sexual corruption I have made known to you about myself. That's excellent! You should find an even greater amount of confident expectation for your own escape from sexual sin.

I hope you will continue reading the balance of this book because in the next chapter I am going to explore some common questions Christian sexual addicts secretly ask within their hearts: *Why am I this way?* and *Is there hope for me?*

As we proceed into the second part of the book (chapters 6-10), I will bear upon four practical daily actions a Christian can develop to detonate the active and operative power of God's Holy Spirit for triumph over sexual addiction.

If you struggle with any measure of persistent compulsive preoccupation toward sexual impurity, this book is for you.

Eleven-year-old John Allen Brown Tap Dancing Photo from Carol Cooper School of Dance, 1977

Thirteen-year-old John Allen Brown Waving to the Camera During Training at the American Musical Theater in Petoskey, Michigan (North Central Michigan College Dormitory in Background), 1979

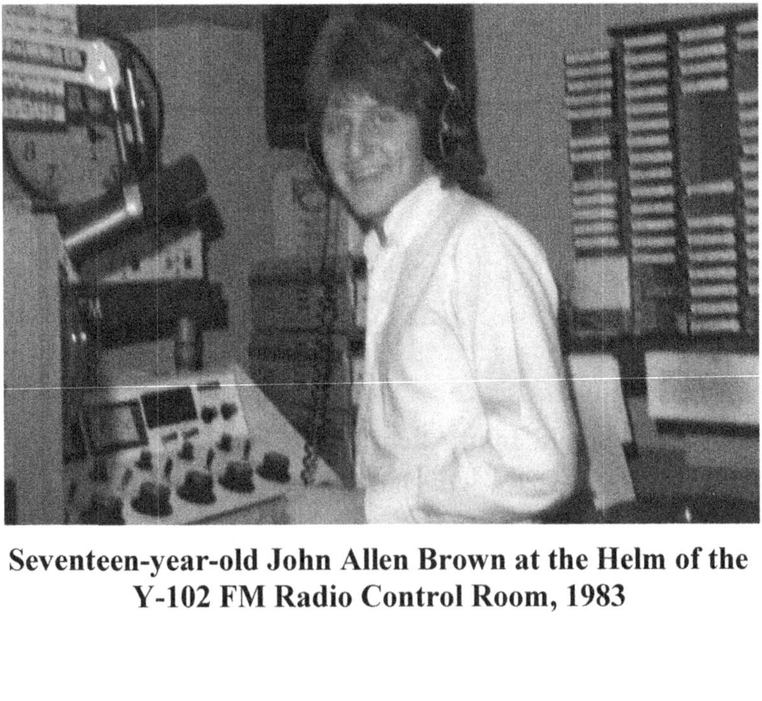

Seventeen-year-old John Allen Brown at the Helm of the Y-102 FM Radio Control Room, 1983

The Incarcerated John Allen Brown Receiving a Visit from His Parents at Buster Cole State Jail, 1995

John Allen Brown Receives a Visit from His Sister, Teri, During His Incarceration at the Maximum Security McConnell Unit, 1999

Preaching the Sunday Morning Service at Unity Baptist Church in Texarkana, Texas, on January 9, 2005

~ Chapter Five ~

The Besetting Sin: Why Am I This Way? Is There Hope for Me?

It's everywhere! It's everywhere! In all reality, a person cannot avoid crossing paths with sexually immoral influences on a frequent basis within twenty-first century culture. I have had to accept the fact that unless I join a monastery and lead a cloistered life severed from general society, I am not going to evade the permeating presence of unprincipled sexual influences.

Sexual immorality has interlaced itself in practically every facet of our American civilization (e.g., fashion trends, television and film, music, literature, advertising, the Internet...*It's everywhere! It's everywhere!*) The presence of sexually immoral influence is clearly gaining ground as evidenced through ongoing destruction of God-honoring, biblical boundaries and a prevailing desensitization of the sensitizing agent of moral conscience.

The good news in all of this is the fact that, in spite of one's inability to evade *all* contact with sexually immoral influences, a Christian *can* escape the power which these immoral influences have on the direction of our thinking and behavior. How does a Christian do this? By the active and operative power of God's Holy Spirit.

Unfortunately there are a great number of Christians who are not successfully escaping the present and prevailing power of sexual immorality within our world. Just as I had done over a period of years, beginning in my childhood, many Christians are incrementally and imperceptibly being desensitized and falling prey to the power of sexual immorality in their thinking and behavior.

SMOKE? WHAT SMOKE?

I used to smoke cigarettes. At one time, I was smoking between four and five packs a day (i.e. chain-smoking). I would wake up in the morning and take my first deep breath of air, only to feel the build-up of tobacco tar splitting apart in my lungs. Of course, as soon as I took that first deep breath of air and coughed really good, I would reach over to the nightstand and fire up a cigarette.

As a smoker, it did not matter how immaculate I cleaned my home, if a non-smoker walked in they could instantly discern that a smoker lived there. It did not matter how well I freshened and deodorized the interior of my car, if a non-smoker got in they could rapidly sense that a smoker owned it. No matter how fragrant the detergent was with which I washed my clothing, no matter how much cologne I bespattered on my skin, a non-smoker could come near and immediately know that I was a smoker.

I, on the other hand, thought my home was purged of the smell of smoke after a good cleaning. I thought for sure my car, clothing, and skin were all purified from the smell of smoke following a good washing and deodorizing. However, the truth of the matter is that my olfactory senses had become desensitized to cigarette smoke because I was constantly in its presence.

Just as the sense organ of our nose is designed to receive stimuli which excite neurons that transmit information to the brain so we can identify a specific smell; likewise, as Christians, when it comes to biblical sexual morality, the sensitizing agent of our moral conscience (in cooperation with the Holy Spirit) is designed to enable us to identify right from wrong according to the absolute standard of God's Word. Furthermore, once the Christian has identified what is right from wrong in any given situation regarding sexuality, the power of God's active and operative Holy Spirit is available to help us live up to the absolute biblical standard.

The problem is that there is a progressive desensitizing effect taking place among many Christians when it comes to our moral conscience and conviction of the Holy Spirit regarding biblical sexual morality. Just as my olfactory senses had become desensitized to cigarette smoke because I was constantly around it, the conviction of our Christian moral conscience can become desensitized to sexual immorality because we are constantly bombarded by its presence in the world around us. If we allow ourselves to get to the place where we are past feeling the conviction of God's Holy Spirit within our Christian moral conscience when it comes to sexual immorality, we are giving ourselves over to the deeper consequences of sexual addiction and its lascivious, unclean, insatiable control:

> *"Who being **past feeling** have given themselves over unto lasciviousness, to work all uncleanness with greediness."*
>
> (Ephesians 4:19)

PRESENT AND PREVAILING

In its proper context, the "besetting sin" referred to in Hebrews 12:1 is the sin of "unbelief".

"...let us lay aside every weight, and the sin which doth so easily beset us,..."

However, there is a principle here which can just as easily apply to any sin that is continually present and prevailing against the Christian. In fact, the adjective *"besetting"* describes quite well the very character of sexual immorality within our world today. In the original Greek, the word *"beset"* has a twofold import: (a) *To have an encircling presence;* (b) *To have an advantage of prevailing against.*

The "besetting sin" of sexual immorality indeed has an *ever-encircling presence* within our culture, and it is increasing in its advantage of *prevailing* against mankind. The present and prevailing nature of sexually immoral influence in our culture is becoming a hindrance to many

Christians, desensitizing their moral conscience, and little by little leading them into the crushing grip of sexual addiction.

THE RACE

> *"...and let us run with patience the race that is set before us."*
>
> (Hebrews 12:1)

How do we begin to navigate the ever-present and prevailing obstacle course of sexually immoral influences? Well, first we need to identify and get rid of any sexually immoral influences within our own sphere of living over which we have control. In order to *"run the race set before us"* we must *"lay aside every weight"*. In other words, I may not have control over all of the sexually immoral influences which I face in the world around me, but some of those "weighty" influences I do have control over. I can control the kind of magazines and books I read, the type of entertainment I watch on television and film, the kind of websites I go to on the Internet, the conversations in which I choose to partake, the circle of friends I choose to have, etc.

The "race" that God has called us to run is the race of holiness (this is not to be confused with the race of "holier than thou" which is built upon religious hypocrisy [see *Isaiah 65:1-5*]).

Fundamentally, holiness signifies separation. That is, separation *to* God and *from* sin.

Positionally speaking, as Christians, we are as "holy" as we ever need to be since it is by Christ's righteousness we are set apart to serve God in eternal right standing.

> *"For God made Christ, who never sinned, to be the offering for our sin, so that we could be made right with God through Christ."*
>
> (2 Corinthians 5:21 [NLT])

> *"I am overwhelmed with joy in the LORD my God! For he has dressed me with the cloth-*

> *ing of salvation and draped me in a robe of righteousness . . ."*
>
> (Isaiah 61:10 [NLT])

In other words, when God looks at a Christian it is not the Christian's righteousness which God sees. Rather, it is Christ's righteousness which He sees. Since Jesus is completely "holy" in all His righteousness, God sees the Christian as completely "holy" because it is Christ's righteousness which is credited to the Christian. There are many people who mistakenly believe that they must maintain their *positional* right-standing with God by their own righteousness:

> *"For they don't understand God's way of making people right with himself. Instead, they are clinging to their own way of getting right with God by trying to keep the law. They won't go along with God's way. For Christ has accomplished the whole purpose of the law. All who believe in him are made right with God."*
>
> (Romans 10:3,4 [NLT])

It is utterly hopeless for a person to attempt using their own righteousness to preserve their positional right standing with God. We are as positionally holy as we will ever need to be because Christ's righteousness was credited to us through saving faith in Him. Since Christ's righteousness is eternally incapable of ever becoming "unrighteous", the born-again believer is eternally secure in Christ's righteousness. Praise God!

PRACTICAL HOLINESS

"Practical holiness" is a different story altogether. Even though we Christians are positionally secure in Christ's perfect holiness, it is still necessary to cooperate with the indwelling Holy Spirit of God by practicing holy living (this is what we refer to as practical holiness). Whereas positional holiness speaks to our deliverance from the eternal penalty of sin, practical holiness speaks to our deliverance from the power of sin:

> *"God wants you to be **holy**, so you should keep clear of all sexual sin ....God has called us to be **holy**, not to live impure lives."*
>
> (1Thessalonians 4:3,7 [NLT])

> *"Having therefore these promises, dearly beloved, let us cleanse ourselves from all filthiness of the flesh and spirit, perfecting **holiness** in the fear of God."*
>
> (2 Corinthians 7:1)

> *"...put on the new man, which after God is created in righteousness and true **holiness.**"*
>
> (Ephesians 4:24)

> *"...what **holy**, godly lives you should be living!"*
>
> (2 Peter 3:11 [NLT])

Do you see all the underlined words in these verses which indicate our cooperation with the Holy Spirit of God when it comes to **practical holiness?**

"Keep clear of"

"Let us cleanse ourselves"

"Put on the new man"

"What holy, godly lives you should be living"

There is practical action involved on our part as Christians when it comes to "laying aside every weight of sin" which causes us to deviate from running the race of holiness. This action (i.e. practical holiness) is necessary on my part if I want the Holy Spirit of God to give me active and operative power over the power of the present and prevailing sexually immoral influences within the world and its misguiding tendency to lead me off course in my thinking and behavior.

The second part of this book is going to carve out the details regarding practical daily actions the Christian sexual addict can develop in order to detonate the ongoing revival of active and operative power of God's Holy Spirit for genuine victory over sexual addiction. Conversely, without learning to develop practical holiness in our lives, we will surely continue to have our moral conscience inconspicuously desensitized by the besetting nature of sexually immoral influences within today's world. As a result, we will continue deviating from the proper path which God has set before us to run the race of holiness.

WHY AM I THIS WAY?

I need to address this question before we go any further. I have met more than several Christians who possess deep-rooted habitual urges toward various forms of sexual immorality. Many of these Christians are extremely reluctant to discuss their propensities because of shame and fear of social stigmata. In fact, I am positive there is an untold amount of Christians who secretly contend with a diversity of sexually immoral tendencies. Some people never act on those tendencies, but many covertly do.

Whether acted upon or not, a Christian's penchant toward specific recurrent sexually immoral desires often causes the Christian to silently believe there must be something especially warped and contaminated deep within himself which will prevent him from ever truly being the full-fledged Christian man which the Lord would have him become. His private self and his public self are out of sync; thus, this leads many Christians to wear the "mask" of spiritual wholeness when, in reality, they are always asking themselves: "*Why am I this way?*"

First of all, let me encourage you to stop believing that you are more warped and contaminated than other Christians. You are far from being alone, my friend. You see, I don't know what your specific sexually immoral struggle may be, but the fact is that you are not especially deviant *just because* you have sexually immoral proclivities.

Please understand that I am not condoning any sexually immoral behavior or excusing a person's personal responsibility concerning their actions; rather, I am only saying you are not alone in your inclinations, and the inclination toward sexual immorality is not itself an *act* of sin.

I want you to understand that your desire, bent, temptation toward any form of sexual immorality does not make you any less valuable in the eyes of God. He still poured out His blood for you! He loves you and has an incredibly wonderful plan and purpose for your life regardless of the sexually immoral proneness with which you are facing. Now, having said that, I want you to recognize that our sexually immoral leanings become sin when we <u>act on them</u> in our thought-life and/or behavior:

> *"But every man is tempted, when he is drawn away of his own lust, and enticed. Then when lust hath conceived, it bringeth forth sin:..."*
>
> (James 1:14,15)

This is why it is so vitally important for the Christian sexual addict to confront and deal with his sexually immoral compulsions instead of "masking" them and keeping them secret.

Back to the question a Christian sexual addict often silently asks himself: *"Why am I this way?"* Well, we could spend time exploring the psychological and environmental influences that our earliest relationships and experiences contributed toward specific sexually immoral patterns with which we battle. We could also give time to researching the biological and genetic factors which possibly hint toward the intrinsic predisposition some people may have with particular sexually immoral desires. However, while all of these influences and factors could be advanced as strong theories (supported by some interesting scientific inquiry) for giving answers to our question of *"Why am I this way?"*, I want to delve deeper into the real primal heart of the problem in answer to that question.

> *"The human **heart** is most deceitful and desperately wicked. Who really knows how bad it is?"*
>
> (Jeremiah 17:9 [NLT])

> *"...for the imagination of man's **heart** is evil from his youth..."*
>
> (Genesis 8:21)

> *"...out of the evil treasure [of the **heart**] bringeth forth evil things."*
>
> (Matthew 12:35) brackets mine

> *"And God saw that the wickedness of man was great in the earth, and that every imagination of the thoughts of his **heart** was only evil continually."*
>
> (Genesis 6:5)

> *"For from the **heart** come...sexual immorality..."*
>
> (Matthew 15:19 [NLT])

All of mankind has an innate predilection toward sin because their "heart" (i.e. their soul) is separated from the life of God by means of spiritual death. This spiritual death took place when mankind's progenitorship—Adam and Eve—died spiritually as a result of disobeying God by eating from the "tree of the knowledge of good and evil." (see *Genesis 2:16,17; 3:1-6*)

You, I, and all of mankind were existent in a dormant sense within the successive generational reproductive totality of Adam's loins. Thus, when Adam sinned, everyone sinned:

> ***"When Adam sinned**, sin entered the entire human race. Adam's sin brought death, so death spread to everyone, for **everyone sinned."***
>
> (Romans 5:12 [NLT])

In other words, mankind's latent existence within the loins of Adam infers our individual participation when he sinned. Hence, we are all born spiritually blind and separated from the life of God, and we possess a propensity to harden our darkened hearts against God:

> *"Their closed minds are full of darkness; they are far away from the life of God because they have shut their minds and hardened their **hearts** against him."*
>
> (Ephesians 4:18 [NLT])

We have a "sin nature"—that is, our "heart" is partisan in allegiance to depravity. We are born enslaved to a depraved heart which incessantly rises up in mutiny against the moral absolutes of God. Accordingly, our depraved heart brings forth depraved behavior which is ultimately self-defeating, self-destructive, and harmful to others. That is the sexual addict's answer to the question: *"Why am I this way?"*

Now someone who has never been in the grip of sexual addiction might say, "John, I've never committed, or even thought about committing some of the shockingly evil sexual transgressions I learn about in the news every day!" We might even hear some sexual addicts comparing their own inclinations with the more vile leanings of other sexual addicts and declaring, "At least I'm not *that* depraved!" Nonetheless, if you are one of those people who has not plunged to the depths of sexually immoral behavior that many others have, it is only because you have not done so *yet.* The capacity for committing the most staggeringly atrocious sexual sin exists within the depraved heart of *every* human being!

It is true that God has hard-wired all mankind with a sense of basic instinctive human morals:

> *"Even when Gentiles, who do not have God's written law,* ***instinctively*** *follow what the law says, they show that* ***in their hearts*** *they know right from wrong."*
>
> (Romans 2:14 [NLT])

Some people are more prone to act upon their instinctive human morals than others; however, *no person* is without a depraved heart and its potential for rabid revolt against God in any area of life at any given moment—including the region of biblical sexual morality.

> *"...we have already shown that* ***all people****, whether Jews or Gentiles, are under the* ***power of sin****. As the Scriptures say,* ***'No one is good—not even one'****."*
>
> (Romans 3:9,10 [NLT])

IS THERE HOPE FOR ME?

Once a sexual addict understands that the original reason he deviates toward specific sexually immoral compulsions is because of the total depravity of his heart, the next logical question would be: *"Is there hope for me?"*

The short answer to that question is: "No! Total depravity of the heart is a hopeless condition in and of itself!"

Now wait a minute. Before you decide to close this book and wander off into the hopelessness of your depraved heart, allow me to give you the protracted answer to that question.

It is true that the sinful nature of man's heart will hopelessly and incessantly propel him to stray from God's moral absolutes; however, God has not abandoned us in the hopeless condition of our depraved hearts unless we choose to remain in such a hopeless condition:

> *"Now the God of hope fill you with all joy and peace in believing,* ***that ye may abound in hope,*** *through the power of the Holy Ghost."*
>
> (Romans 15:13)

Our hope for overcoming the depravity of our heart comes from *the God of hope*! It is through *believing* in the "God of hope"—that is, active faith in Jesus Christ as Lord and Savior—that the sexual addict may *abound in hope* that God's promises include victory over the power of one's sin nature (which encompasses sexually immoral compulsions that have previously enslaved you).

By the way, the kind of hope we are talking about is not the kind of hope we would use if we said: "I hope the sky will be sunny and blue next week." That kind of hope leaves room for doubt. Rather, the kind of *hope* which originates from *the God of hope* is a hope of **confident expectation.** In other words, God's promises to the Christian are unable to fail! When we receive Jesus Christ as personal Lord and Savior, the abounding hope we experience in believing (i.e. active faith) is a confident expectation that God's promises will be actualized in our lives without fail. That includes the promise of *Romans 6:6*:

> *"Our old sinful selves were crucified with Christ so that sin might lose its power in our lives. We are no longer slaves to sin."*
>
> (Romans 6:6 [NLT])

The fact that God promises we are no longer slaves to sin because of saving faith in Jesus Christ is a fact that should bring abounding hope when it comes to the hopeless condition of our depraved heart!

Notice the last seven words of Romans 15:13:

> *"...through the power of the Holy Ghost."*

The actualization of God's promises in our lives is accomplished *through the power of the Holy Ghost.* Be patient with me for a few minutes and let me explain how this happens. It is important for you to understand this if you want to walk in victory over sexual addiction.

When a sinner exercises saving faith in Jesus Christ as their Lord and Savior, that sinner becomes a Christian and experiences *regeneration*:

> *"Not by works of righteousness which we have done, but according to [God's] mercy he saved us, by the washing of* ***regeneration****, and renewing* ***[through] the Holy Ghost.****"*
> (Titus 3:5 [brackets mine])

Stay with me here and pay close attention to what I am about to write. As we have already established, mankind was separated from the spiritual life of God in the Garden of Eden. This, of course, left mankind enslaved to a depraved heart which innately rebels against the moral absolutes of God. However, through saving faith in Jesus Christ, mankind can now be reunited with the life of God and experience the literal indwelling of God's Holy Spirit. This is called "spiritual *regeneration*" or what is commonly referred to as being "born again." [Note: The Greek word for "regeneration" is *paliggenesia.* It is a compound of the words *palin*, meaning "again", and *genesis*, meaning "birth"—being born again—is specifically referring to the emergence of a "new nature" in contrast with the "sin nature".]

This "new nature" experienced by a Christian is the actual resurrection life and power of Jesus Christ by the indwelling of the Holy Spirit of God within our human spirit and soul:

> *"I pray that you will begin to understand the incredible greatness of [God's] power for us who believe in him. This is the same mighty power that raised Christ from the dead and*

seated him in the place of honor at God's right hand in the heavenly realms."
(Ephesians 1:19, 20 [NLT] brackets mine)

Please listen closely. This "new nature" of Christ's resurrection life and power within us, via the indwelling Holy Spirit, offers us an *option* to live victoriously over our sin nature" (i.e., proclivity toward sin) which still exists within the Christian but has lost its inescapable and positional authority over the Christian's life now that "spiritual regeneration" has occurred with the indwelling of God's Holy Spirit. In other words:

"...you have no obligation whatsoever to do what your sinful nature urges you to do."
(Romans 8:12 [NLT])

You now have a "new nature" from which you can choose to live your life in the victorious power of God's Holy Spirit:

"Before, you let yourselves be slaves of impurity and lawlessness. Now you must ***choose*** *to be slaves of righteousness so that you will become holy."*
(Romans 6:19 [NLT])

AN ONGOING REVIVAL OF POWER

Looking back at *Titus 3:5* we see it not only mentions that the Christian has been saved by *"...the washing of regeneration,"* but it also says we have been saved by the ***"renewing** of the Holy Ghost."* I want you to understand that we have not only been regenerated (i.e. born again) and experienced the inception of a new nature, but there is also a **renewing** which begins to take place within the Christian's life through the Holy Spirit.

One of the main differences between *regeneration* and *renewing* is the fact that the regeneration experience is a once-for-all occurrence. In other words when you are born again by grace through faith in Jesus Christ and receive the indwelling Holy Spirit of God, you are secure *in* your salvation. You are *in* Christ Jesus' righteousness, positionally speaking. You have been positionally delivered from citizenship of one domain (i.e. the domain of darkness) and you have positionally become a citizen of another domain (i.e. the domain of light):

> *"For he has rescued us from the one who rules in the kingdom of darkness, and he has brought us into the kingdom of his dear Son."*
>
> (Colossians 1:13 [NLT])

We have been positionally delivered from the judicial penalty of sin (i.e. death [separation from the life of God]), and we have been positionally brought into eternal life with God. In fact, Jesus said:

> *"I assure you, those who listen to my message and believe in God who sent me have eternal life. They will never be condemned for their sins, but they have already passed from death into life."*
>
> (John 5:24 [NLT])

This regeneration experience is a once-for-all occurrence. The Holy Spirit accomplishes this when we receive Jesus Christ as Lord and Savior.

Distinct from regeneration, however, is the renewing process, mentioned in *Titus 3:5*, which is not a once-for-all occurrence but is an ever-advancing and developing result of being born again. The original Greek word for renewing means that, little by little, there is a transformation and renovation within the Christian heart (i.e. soul) which adapts his thinking to that of the mind of Christ. It is through this renewing process that the Christian is empowered by the Holy Spirit of God to live victorious over sin, and function as a citizen of the kingdom of God on earth.

This renewing process is the hope we can have for deliverance from any form of sexual addiction. However, it is critical to understand that the renewing process requires the Christian's active cooperation with the Holy Spirit through practical holiness on a daily basis. It is only by choosing to actively cooperate with the Holy Spirit through daily practical holiness that our new nature gives us access to the ongoing revival of God's Holy Spirit power which we need.

Remember, if the Christian sexual addict refuses to actively cooperate with God through practical holiness on a daily basis, the renewing process toward Christlikeness will be obstructed, and the ongoing revival of God's Holy Spirit power will be suppressed. The natural consequence of this will be a conquest of the Christian's thinking and behavior by his sin nature. A desensitizing effect will increasingly take place within the moral conscience concerning sexual immorality because of its ever-present and prevailing influence in the world around us. The besetting sin of sexual addiction will flourish in the Christian's life as he gives himself over to the deeper ramifications of compulsive sexual behavior and its lascivious, unclean, insatiable control.

The choices are clear: A Christian sexual addict can either *choose* to actively cooperate with Christ through "practical holiness" on a daily basis, and allow the ongoing revival of God's Holy Spirit to empower him so he can have his thinking progressively adapted to the mind of Christ-likeness and live in victory over the persistent compulsive preoccupation with sexual immorality; or, he can *choose* to refuse actively cooperating with Jesus through daily practical holiness and allow his sin nature to continue dominating his thinking and behavior. What will be your choice?

TOTALLY COMMITTED

If you are ready to detonate the active and operative power of God's Holy Spirit in your life through practical holiness, it is going to take total commitment. Jesus has made a total commitment "*...even further by dying a criminal's death on a cross.*" (Philippians 2:8 [NLT])

Total commitment means we are to give our bodies and minds to God "*...Let them be a living and holy sacrifice—the kind he will accept. When you think of what he has done for you, is this too much to ask?*" (Romans 12:1 [NLT])

A total commitment to Jesus is demonstrated in our active cooperation with Him through practical holiness on a daily basis. The practical applications of holiness which are explained within the remaining chapters of this book will require your total commitment if you wish to experience a new level of freedom from sexual addiction. Your total commitment to the following practical daily actions will bring about an ongoing revival of Holy Spirit power as you experience the renewing resurrection life and power of Jesus Christ flowing through your soul, transforming your spiritual mind to the mind of Christlikeness. Are you truly ready to escape the besetting sin of sexual addiction? Then give your total commitment to the practical applications of holiness you will study in the balance of this book.

> *"He gave his life to free us from every kind of sin, to cleanse us, and to make us his very own people,* ***totally committed*** *to doing what is right."*
>
> (Titus 2:14 [NLT])

A QUICK NOTE

In the event that you are reading this book and have never truly received Jesus Christ as your Lord and Savior, I want you to understand that the following applications of practical holiness in the remaining chapters will do very little to help you gain and maintain victory over sexual addiction. It will be kind of like lighting the fuse on a stick of dynamite which contains no explosive—sure, the fuse is combustible and makes a sizzling sound as it burns its way toward detonation, only to fizzle out because the stick of dynamite is a powerless dud. You see, without the explosive resurrection power of God's indwelling Holy Spirit, the practical applications on the following pages are nothing more than a powerless dud.

Will you receive Jesus Christ as your Lord and Savior right now? Slowly consider each line of the following prayer until you can mean it from your heart. God is listening.

"Heavenly Father, in the authority of Jesus name, I pray this prayer because I know beyond a doubt that I am separated from the life of God. I also acknowledge that without your indwelling resurrection life and power, my old sinful nature has authority over my life and I will never have true victory over the sexual addiction which enslaves my mind. I also understand that Jesus is the only way to genuine salvation, and to reject Jesus Christ is the basis for eternal condemnation in hell. Lord, I no longer want to live as a condemned sinner in a hopeless condition, separated from the life of Jesus Christ. Please, as I acknowledge my total depravity of heart, I turn from sin and turn to you through faith, believing that you will indwell me with your Holy Spirit, giving me a new nature as a child of God. I call on you Jesus! Save my soul from the penalty of sin, and begin the renewing process of transforming me into Christlikeness. I am now totally committed to you. As I study the remainder of this book, and as I wholeheartedly exercise the practical applications of holiness, allow me to experience the explosive ongoing revival of your Holy Spirit power in my life. Give me victory over my sin nature and the sexual addiction with which I contend. Thank you, Lord Jesus, for saving my soul!

Amen."

If you said that prayer from your heart, Welcome to the family of God! It is important that you find a mature

Christian and tell them that you have received Jesus Christ as your Lord and Savior! Praise God!

Okay, here we go…let's light the fuse as we move toward detonating the active and operative power of God's Holy Spirit in our lives through *four applications of practical holiness.*

PART TWO

Four Applications of Practical Holiness

"As we know Jesus better, his divine power
gives us everything we need for
living a godly life. He has called us to receive his
own glory and goodness!
And by that same mighty power, he has
given us all of his rich and wonderful promises.
He has promised that you will escape
the decadence all around you caused
by evil desires and that you will share in his
divine nature. So make every effort to apply the
benefits of these promises to your life.
Then your faith will produce
a life of moral excellence.
A life of moral excellence leads to
knowing God better."

(2 Peter 1:3-5 [NLT])

~ Chapter Six ~

Transparent Honesty/Accountability

Practical Application # 1: Be transparently honest with yourself, God, and another Christian about your deepest sexual frailties and weaknesses; then, maintain an accountability friendship.

Who really wants to admit they have sinful sexual urges and behavior which are kept hidden from other people? In reality I have met numerous people—mostly those who have had legal problems as a repercussion of illicit sexual actions—who humbly acknowledge they struggled with entrenched sexually immoral compulsions long before they ended up dealing with the harsh consequences. Now, through enforced humility, many of these people (including myself) wish we had been transparently honest with someone about our struggles and gotten the help we needed before finding ourselves standing in front of a judge facing probation, prison time, or registration as a sex offender.

Maybe you are one of those people who have found themselves in legal trouble because of aberrant sexual behavior. Maybe you are not doing any illegal sexual activity, yet you still contend with a persistent compulsive preoccupation toward sexual gratification. Perhaps you are doing (or contemplating) sexually immoral things about which you would never want to tell anyone else. Why? I mean, why would you not want to tell anyone else? I'll tell you why: **Shame.**

SHAME! SHAME! SHAME!

I do not claim to be a "Dr. James Dobson" by any means. However, I once took a college course in business psychology. One thing I especially remember most about the series of lessons we studied is that a person's *self-esteem* affects their *self-concept*, which in turn, affects their *self-confidence*. For clarity purposes, let me briefly define these three things which deal with "self":

Self-Esteem: A person's sense of estimable value as a human being. In other words, how much realistic respect a person has for oneself.

Self-Concept: How a person conceives or thinks of oneself in comparison to other human beings: self-image.

Self-Confidence: How sure a person feels about his ability to function successfully as a human being.

These three things are interrelated in such a way that if a person's *self-esteem* is negatively affected and they lose a sense of respect for themselves as a person, their *self-concept* is automatically affected in a negative manner. By natural default, their *self-confidence* is negatively impacted as well and a guilty shame begins to dominate their lives.

We live in a world that places massive emphasis on a person's estimable worth as a human being. If a person does something to lose the respect of society, he is essentially marginalized as someone who has no central importance, he becomes somewhat of a "social leper" in the eyes of others.

This could not be more true when it comes to sexual transgressions. Although our American culture is replete with the promotion of sexual immorality and perversion, that very same culture is quick to ostracize a person who has "crossed the line" when it comes to certain sexual sins. [Note: At the writing of this book, the *U.S. Department of Justice Sex Offender Registry* has the names of close to 550,000 people who have been charged with or convicted of sexual crimes]. The irony of it all is that our sex-saturated culture, which is so quick to condemn the sexual addict, is the external impetus which feeds the internal compulsivity of the sexual addict.

If it sounds like I am trying to minimize the sexual addict's behavior and responsibility, I am not. Every human being who struggles with a persistent compulsive preoccupation toward sexually immoral behavior *must* take personal responsibility for his actions. In essence, that is what this book is about—helping the sexual addict acknowledge the seriousness of his problem and to take specific biblically-based actions for escaping the driving compulsion of sexually immoral thoughts and behavior. However, the point I am attempting to stress at this moment in the book is the fact that a very large number of people who battle sexually immoral urges and behavior will choose to remain silent about their struggles because their *self-esteem* is already damaged by the shame they are carrying around as a result of the respect they have lost for themselves; inferentially, their *self-concept* and *self-confidence* are also greatly diminished. To the sexual addict, the very suggestion of letting anyone else find out about his sexually immoral inclinations is a threat to any remaining vestige of self-esteem he is trying to hang onto, especially in light of the condemning social climate toward sexual offenses.

There is a highly probable chance that an extremely large number of people with whom you come in contact may very likely be hiding a secret shame with compulsive sexual behavior because they do not wish to experience any further shame or loss of respect imposed by society. Nevertheless, it is only when the sexual addict becomes *transparently honest* with himself, God, and another Christian that victory over sexual sin, and genuine freedom from shame can be experienced:

> *"People who cover over their sins will not prosper. But if they confess and forsake them, they will receive mercy."*
>
> (Proverbs 28:13 [NLT])

IN THE GARDEN

Husband and wife. Adam and Eve in the garden eastward in Eden. We read the record in *Genesis:*

> *"Now, although Adam and his wife were both naked, neither of them felt any shame."*
> (2:25 [NLT])

The word *"shame"* in that verse comes from the original Hebrew which has overtones of feeling "worthless". The verse clearly reveals that Adam and Eve had *no* feelings of shame (i.e., no feelings of worthlessness). They had a wonderful sense of *self-esteem.* Why did they have such a perfect respect and sense of worth about themselves? Well, take another look at the verse. It also informs us that Adam and Eve were "naked". It is true that they were physically naked; however, I believe there is a layer of spiritual truth implied here as well—that is, they were also "naked" in the sense that they had nothing immoral to hide. Praise God! When a person has nothing immoral to hide, he has nothing to be ashamed of!

Because Adam and Eve had nothing to hide, they were able to have a perfect respect and sense of worth about themselves. They were even able to have perfect fellowship with their Lord and Creator God with whom they took walks in the garden. Oh, to walk with God in intimate fellowship as His children. No wonder their self-esteem was without shame—their sense of worth was rooted in the fact that they were created in God's very image (see *Genesis 1:27*). They walked with Him in shameless, sinless fellowship as His children.

UH—OH!

As part of a morning radio show I once hosted, there was a segment called Today in History. For instance, I might say: "Today in history, January 22, 1973, the U.S. Supreme Court ruled 7-2, in Roe v. Wade, that states may not ban abortions during the first trimester of pregnancy and may regulate, but not ban, abortions during the second trimester of pregnancy."

Or perhaps, I would say: "Today in history, July 16, 1945, the very first atomic bomb was manufactured at Los Alamos, New Mexico."

There is one day in history I never talked about on the radio which negatively impacted mankind more significantly than any other day. We don't seem to note it very often as a day that altered the course of the entire world and humanity, but it did. What took place on that day in history dealt a death blow to every human being who has lived, does live, or will ever live.

We first find that day in history mentioned in Genesis:

> *"And the LORD God took the man, and put him into the garden of Eden to dress it and to keep it. And the LORD God commanded the man, saying, Of every tree of the garden thou mayest freely eat: But of the tree of the knowledge of good and evil, thou shalt not eat of it: for in the day that thou eatest thereof thou shalt surely die."*
>
> (2:15-17)

Notice it says "*in the day*". I don't know the exact day it was, but "*in [that] day*" when Eve was deceived by Satan and transgressed into sin, and Adam willfully went along with her as they ate of the forbidden fruit from the *"tree of the knowledge of good and evil"*, that was "the day in history" which negatively impacted mankind more significantly than any other day in history. (see *Genesis 3:1-6; 1 Timothy 2:13,14*).

We read in *Genesis 3:7* what happened in that day when Adam and Eve sinned against God by disobeying his instructions:

> *"At that moment, their eyes were opened, and they suddenly* ***felt shame*** *at their nakedness.*

> *So they strung fig leaves together around their hips to cover themselves."* (NLT)

Notice that after Adam and Eve ate of the forbidden fruit they *"felt shame"* (i.e. worthlessness). They lost respect for themselves as their self-esteem was diminished. What was the first thing they did when Eve was deceived as the shame set in? Yep, they sewed some leaves together to wear in an effort to cover their shame.

As the cool of that fateful day began to descend on the garden, the Lord came for His evening walk with Adam and Eve. I can imagine it was always a great pleasure for our Lord to walk in loving communion through that beautiful garden with His children on numerous occasions. He loved them so very much, and He loved to be loved by them. It is easy for me to envision that on each evening as Adam and Eve heard the Lord walking in the garden, they would run to Him and hug Him. I can see the big grin on His face and hear the joyful chortle of His voice as He felt the love and companionship of His children.

Something was different on this particular evening. As the Lord walked through the garden, Adam and Eve did not come running to give Him a hug and walk with Him. Our biblical record doesn't say, but I can picture in my mind that perhaps tears were streaming down the Lord's face because, in His all-knowing heart, He already understood what was really going on.

CAMOUFLAGE

Have you ever gone hunting for deer or some other wildlife food? If so, you have probably worn camouflage clothing. Camouflage clothing is fashioned to look like leaves and the bark of trees so the hunter can easily blend in with the wooded surroundings where he is hunting. The better he blends in, the less likely he will be spotted.

Think about what Adam and Eve were doing. They were the first people to ever wear camouflage clothing and try to blend in with the trees:

> *"Toward evening they heard the LORD God walking about in the garden, so they hid themselves among the trees."*
>
> (Genesis3:8 [NLT])

They had strung some fig leaves together as clothing and then *"hid themselves among the trees."* They were ashamed of themselves and surely did not want to fellowship with God after what they had done. So they tried to blend in with the trees and avoid His presence.

We have a tendency to do the same thing when it comes to our wounded self-esteem and sense of shame associated with sexual addiction. We try to camouflage the shame and blend in with the "trees of pretense" so we can hide what is really going on in our lives. People may look at us and see the perfect parent, employee, church member, productive citizen of society; however, underneath all the camouflage, we are struggling with secret and powerful sexually immoral compulsions about which we are ashamed to admit.

AN EXIT RAMP

Admitting our deepest sexual frailties and weaknesses to *ourselves, God, and another Christian* is contrary to our sense of self-esteem. However, the paradox of it all is that God's enabling power within us becomes active and operative when we acknowledge our disabling weaknesses. In fact, Jesus says:

> *"...My grace [favor of enabling power] is sufficient for thee: for my strength is made perfect in weakness..."*
>
> (2 Corinthians 12:9 [brackets mine])

God's desire is that we have complete victory over sexually immoral temptations. Praise God! He is more than willing to provide the active and operative Holy Spirit power necessary for having such victory.

Let us take a look at *1 Corinthians 10.* In *verses 6-10* we read about the Israelites and their downfall in the wilderness journey. Their self-indulgence and lack of self-control brought fatal consequences into their lives. Take special note of *verse 8—*

> *"And we must not engage in sexual immorality as some of them did, causing 23,000 of them to die in one day."* (NLT)

Also, *verse 6* tells us:

> *"These events happened as a warning to us, so that we would not crave evil things as they did."* (NLT)

God very obviously takes sexual immorality extremely serious and we can *expect* negative consequences to befall us when we choose to ignore His warnings.

Some of you may be saying, "But, John, you just don't understand how intense and persistent my obsession toward sexual temptation is at times!" Well, believe me, I do understand. I also understand that the active and operative power of God's Holy Spirit is available to give us victory over the intensity of sexual temptation.

Take a look at *1 Corinthians 10* once again. What does *verse 13* promise us?

> *"But remember that the temptations that come into your life are no different from what others experience. And God is faithful. He will keep the temptation from becoming so strong that you can't stand up against it. When you are tempted, he will show you a way out so that you will not give in to it."*
>
> (NLT)

First of all, this verse tells me that no matter what kind of sexual temptations you and I struggle with, they are no different than what multitudes of humans have contended with since sin entered the world. The phrase: "*the temptations...are no different from what others experience...*" is translated in part from an original Greek word which means "*belonging to human*". In other words, no matter how twisted or shockingly evil your sexually immoral proclivities might be, they just belong to being human. You are not unique in your struggles; there are countless other Christians who deal with the very same compulsions as yourself. Because of the shame associated with those compulsions, most people are afraid to admit their struggles; nonetheless, I assure you, *you are not alone.*

Continuing to look at 1 Corinthians 10:13, the verse also tells us that: "*...God is faithful. He will keep the temptation from becoming so strong that you can't stand up against it...*"

When it says, *"God is faithful"*, that means He can be trusted to do what He says He will do—His promises cannot fail! In this case, God promises to keep the temptation from being too strong for you to resist.

Now anyone who has been enslaved by sexual addiction knows how overpowering sexual temptation can become. There are times when the force of sexual temptation can be so intense that the addict loses all defense and fear of consequences connected to his behavior. The sexually immoral actions of the addict become compulsory as dictated by his "sin nature" and lack of power to resist. My friend, this is a scary place to be. Yet, for the Christian, God promises to keep sexual temptation from becoming so strong that you can't resist it.

How exactly does God keep the sexual addict from giving in to the power of temptation? It is found right there in *1 Corinthians 10:13:*

> *"...When you are tempted, he will show you a way out so that you will not give in to it."*
> (NLT)

Notice it says, *"...he will show you a way out..."* The words *"a way out"* are translated from the Greek word *ekbasis*. That word means *"exit"*.

Imagine, if you will, you are driving down a five-lane interstate in 5 p.m. rush hour traffic. You happen to be traveling in the center lane with cars and trucks in front of you, beside you, behind you. Since it is rush hour, the momentum of all the vehicles is about 85 mph. You begin to notice your exit ramp is rapidly approaching, so you start attempting to navigate your vehicle toward the far right lane. You activate your blinker to signal your intentions to the vehicles in the lane beside you and behind you. To no avail, the vehicles ignore you and do not yield an inch.

Your exit ramp is getting closer. You continue to try and maneuver into the lane to your right. Still no cooperation from the heavy, speeding traffic. Your exit ramp is getting even closer...closer...closer...gone! You've missed your exit and now you'll have to take the long way home.

The ensnaring drive of sexual temptation has a lot of similarities with the preceding illustration. For instance, the sexual addict can be heading in the right direction in life and all of a sudden find ourselves trapped in the unyielding velocity of sexually immoral compulsions. We know we need to "exit" those temptations, but find ourselves completely powerless to the driving force. We make some vain attempts to get on another path but find ourselves dragged away down a road we really did not want to travel. For me, and many others, that road led to prison and *the long way home.*

Now, envision yourself once again on that same interstate during 5 p.m. rush hour traffic. You are once again trapped in the center lane as traffic fails to yield to your attempts at navigating toward the far right lane. Your exit ramp is getting closer. Except, *this time*, out of nowhere, the center lane in which you are traveling miraculously transforms into an exit ramp, and you are able to escape the velocity of traffic to arrive safely home. Wow! Wouldn't that be great?!

That is exactly what God promised to do when it comes to escaping the besetting sin of sexual addiction. When He says He will *"...show you a way out..."* (the KJV says He will *"...make a way of escape..."*) , it means He will make an "exit" ramp for you so the temptation will not be too strong for you to resist. Yes, before you become defeated by the compulsory power of your "sin nature" and its sexually immoral urges, God will make an "exit ramp" for the Christian to take as a path of escape.

I am persuaded to believe that the "exit ramp" God most commonly makes available to the Christian who struggles with compulsive sexual behavior is the "exit ramp" of *transparent honesty* and *accountability.* Let me give you a personal example of what I am talking about. As I mentioned in a previous chapter of this book, I had become addicted to Internet pornography. Even as a Christian, I had allowed myself to give in to the lure of Internet porn and could not seem to escape the dominion it had on my mind. Well, a couple of weeks before I found myself in trouble with the law for accessing images of females under eighteen years old, God had offered me an "exit ramp" via *transparent honesty.* I did not see it as that at the time, but now that I look back I can recognize it for what it was.

Alone at the radio station where I was employed, I sat in front of a computer viewing pornographic websites. My cell phone rang and I noticed the caller identification indicated that the person calling was a Christian friend. I answered the phone and we began conversing. My Christian friend had no idea that I was having any kind of problem with pornography. In fact, my friend had no idea I even looked at pornography at all. However, after we had been talking for a few minutes my friend said, "John, you sound different today. Are you looking at Internet pornography?"

I could not believe what my friend had just asked me! It startled me so much that I turned to look around the room as if someone was watching me. However, by placing it on my friend's heart to ask such a question, God was providing me an "exit ramp" of *transparent honesty* that I could use to escape the power that Internet porn had gotten on my mind. All I had to do at that moment was honestly answer my Christian friend's question by saying, "Yes, I am looking at Internet pornography and it has gained control of my mind."

Had I said those words, I have no doubt that my transparent confession of sin would have made a way for the power of God's Holy Spirit to begin enabling me in resisting going any further into the downward spiral on which I found myself plunging. I wish I had taken that "exit ramp" of transparent honesty, but I did not. Instead, I was ashamed and afraid of losing my friend's respect so I hid my struggle and ended up in jail two weeks later.

By the way, I have since told my Christian friend about what I was doing that day when my cell phone rang. My friend has assured me that there would not have been a loss of respect had I been transparently honest. In fact, my friend tells me that my honesty would ultimately have *increased* their respect for me because of the courage and humility it takes to admit such a struggle.

BACK IN THE GARDEN

As Adam and Eve wore their camouflage clothing and hid among the trees when they heard the Lord arrive for His evening walk, we know that the Lord already understood what His children had done because the Bible teaches us that one of God's attributes is His omniscience (i.e., complete knowledge). God knew that Adam and Eve had sinned. God knew they were trying to cover their shame. God knew they were hiding among the trees. God knew exactly where they were and what was going on. Yet when we look at the biblical record in *Genesis*, what are the first words we hear our Lord say to Adam and Eve on that day in history?

> *"The LORD God called to Adam, 'Where are you?'"*
>
> (Genesis 3:9 [NLT])

By asking this question, God was offering Adam and Eve an "exit ramp" of escape from the sin and shame that had gained dominion upon their lives. The escape God was making available was the "exit ramp" of *transparent honesty.*

The "exit ramp" of transparent honesty has three levels of honesty: 1. *Honesty with yourself;* 2. *Honesty with God;* and 3. *Honesty with another Christian.*

1. Honesty with yourself

God asks Adam a question: *"Where are you?"* As we have previously established, God already knew the answer to that question. The Lord was not asking such a question for His own benefit; rather, God was asking the question for Adam's benefit. God was leading Adam in the direction of self-examination.

Getting honest with ourselves about *"Where we are"* in regard to sexual addiction and how it ruptures and breaks our fellowship with God is the first level of transparent honesty that is needed if we are to eventually experience victory in this area of our life. I need to be transparently honest about "Where I am" when it comes to sexually immoral inclinations:

- "Where am I" when it comes to the specific sexually immoral desires toward which I lean?
- "Where am I" when it comes to the sexually provocative images on which I allow my eyes to dwell?
- "Where am I" when it comes to my obedience to God's expressed will concerning biblical sexuality?

- "Where am I" with my underlying motives concerning potentially vulnerable situations in which I find myself tempted?
- "Where am I?"...am I in God's will or am I out of God's will?

If I can be transparently honest with myself about "Where I am" concerning my sexually immoral struggles, then it is a starting point for the active and operative power of God to get me where I need to be in my daily walk with Him, and victory over sexual sin.

2. Honesty with God

One of the other questions God asks Adam is:

> *"...Have you eaten the fruit I commanded you not to eat?"*
>
> (Genesis 3:11 [NLT])

Again, God knew the answer to this inquiry. The question was asked in an effort to lead Adam in the direction of transparent honesty and confession of sin to his Lord.

Adam's response was an example of what many of us tend to do when confronted with accepting responsibility for our actions:

> *"And the man said, the woman whom thou gavest to be with me, she gave me of the tree, and I did eat"*
>
> (Genesis 3:12)

Instead of simply saying, *"I did eat",* Adam chose to shift some of the responsibility of his sin onto the Lord by pointing out to God *". . . it was the woman **you gave me** who brought me the fruit . . ."* (NLT)

It is easy to shift the blame to other influences and factors when it comes to being transparently honest with God about our immoral sexual behavior. We might say, "God, it is your fault you allowed me to have certain inherent proclivities toward sexual immorality!" We might say: "If only so-and-so had not molested me!"; or "The culture I grew up with promoted sexual immorality and led me to do the ungodly things I have done!"

The list of ways we could shift the blame for our compulsive sexual behavior is ad infinitum. Although the factors and influences we listed may have indeed attributed to our sexually immoral behavior, God just wants us to accept the responsibility for our sin and honestly confess, "I did eat. Yes, Lord, I did eat of the forbidden fruit of sexual immorality, and without the active and operative power of your Holy Spirit, I will continue to be controlled by the power of sexual addiction!"

Remaining transparent with God about our deepest sexual frailties and weaknesses is so vital in escaping the besetting sin of sexual addiction. When we are honest with God about our struggles and admit our complete dependence upon His power to give us victory, we are giving Him free reign to search our hearts and motives for those deep-rooted iniquities which only He can bring to our attention before we are led down the wrong path again:

> *"Search me, O God, and know my heart; test me and know my thoughts. Point out anything in me that offends you, and lead me along the path of everlasting life."*
>
> (Psalm 139:23,24 [NLT])

> *"O, what joy for those whose rebellion is forgiven, whose sin is put out of sight! Yes, what joy for those whose record the LORD has cleared of sin, whose lives are lived in* ***complete honesty****! When I refused to confess my sin, I was weak and miserable, and I groaned all day long. Day and night your hand of discipline was heavy on me. My strength evaporated like water in the summer heat. Finally,* ***I confessed all my sins to you*** *and* ***stopped trying to hide them.*** *I said to*

> *myself, 'I will confess my rebellion to the LORD.' And you forgave me! All my guilt is gone."*
>
> (Psalm 32:1-5 [NLT])

3. Honesty with another Christian

We have discussed two levels of honesty which construct the "exit ramp" of transparent honesty: *Honesty with yourself;* and *Honesty with God.* Let us now examine the third and final level of transparent honesty: *Honesty with another Christian.*

When I use the word transparent in connection to honesty, I am implying that you be very specific about the nature of your sexually immoral struggles. For instance, if you struggle with a persistent compulsive preoccupation toward swimsuit advertisements in the newspaper, be specific about that fact when confessing your struggles to another Christian. Perhaps you contend with Internet porn, same sex attraction, paraphilias (e.g., voyeurism, fetishism, sadism, masochism, pedophilia, exhibitionism, etc.) or any number of the manifestations of sexual immorality. Whatever your struggle, be *specific* about the nature of those struggles. Keep in mind that whatever the sexual temptations are with which you contend:

> *"...the temptations that come into your life are no different from what others experience..."*
>
> (1 Corinthians10:13 [NLT])

You are not alone in your battle. There are countless other Christians who combat the *very same* compulsions with their sinful nature as yourself. Please, do not allow the shame associated with your sexually immoral desires to prevent you from being transparently honest with another Christian. *This is the* ***only*** *way accountability can be maintained,* and the active and operative power of God can flow freely into your soul.

I emphasize "transparency" here because it is easier to be specific about our sexual addiction when being honest with ourselves and God than it is to be specific with another Christian. We might find it much less humbling to simply admit in a "general" way that we struggle with sexual temptations rather than getting specific about the *exact nature* of our temptations.

For some of us our deepest sexual frailties and weaknesses can be very ugly. We would just prefer to bury those ugly sexual tendencies deeper than we bury some of the more "socially acceptable" sexual sins.

I am reminded of a man named Achan. He was the Israeli warrior who disobeyed God by taking loot from a city the Israelites were to completely destroy in battle. Achan's sin was a hindrance to any further victory for Israel until the sin was dealt with.

> *"Then Joshua said to Achan, 'My son, give glory to the LORD, the God of Israel by telling the truth. Make your confession and tell me what you have done. Don't hide it from me.' Achan replied, 'I have sinned against the LORD, the God of Israel. For I saw a beautiful robe imported from Babylon, two hundred silver coins, and a bar of gold weighing more than a pound. I wanted them so much that I took them. They are hidden in the ground beneath my tent, with the silver buried deeper than the rest."*
>
> (Joshua 7:19-21 [NLT])

Notice, Achan begins his confession to Joshua in *verse 20, "...I have sinned against the LORD, the God of Israel"* (NLT) That was certainly a confession of sin. However, it wasn't very specific. Achan's transparency actually begins in *verse 21, "For I saw a beautiful robe imported from Babylon, two hundred silver coins, and a bar of gold weighing more than a pound. I wanted them so much that I took them. They are hidden in the ground beneath my tent..."*(NLT) Now that was being very specific.

If we pay close attention to this verse, we will also notice that Achan could simply have told Joshua about the robe and the gold without ever mentioning the silver because *"...the silver [is] buried* ***deeper*** *than the rest."*

There is an interesting parallel I would like to advance at this point. All of this loot was buried in the ground beneath Achan's tent. Well, the Bible has a couple of places where it uses the word "tent" figuratively in referring to our body. One of those places is 2 Corinthians 5:1:

> *"For we know that when this earthly* ***tent*** *we live in is taken down—when we die and leave these bodies—we will have a home in heaven, an eternal body made for us by God himself and not by human hands."* (NLT)

Just as Achan tried to hide his sin by burying the forbidden items inside his tent, we too bury our forbidden sexual compulsions inside our "earthly tents" (i.e., our bodies—more specifically, our hearts). Just like Achan, we bury some of the forbidden items **deeper** than the rest.

It is extremely important that we be transparently honest about our **deepest** sexual frailties and weaknesses. *Otherwise, maintaining an accountability relationship with another Christian will be impossible.* Additionally, just as Achan's sin hindered Israel from further victory in battle, if we keep our sexual sin buried in our heart, we will fail to experience victory in our battle against the besetting sin of sexual addiction.

NO STEEPLE CLIMBING REQUIRED

Now please do not panic when I tell you how important it is to be *transparently honest* with another Christian about your deepest sexual frailties and weaknesses. I am not suggesting that you climb to the apex of the church steeple with a megaphone in hand and announce to the world your sexual struggles. There is no reason to disclose this information to all people.

What I am suggesting you do is find at least two Christian men [if you are a female you should seek out two Christian women] who are wise, mature, and solid in their walk with Christ Jesus.

> *"A person standing alone can be attacked and defeated, but two can stand back-to-back and conquer. Three are even better, for a triple-braided cord is not easily broken."*
> (Ecclesiastes 4:12 [NLT])

If you are unsure about whom you can be transparently honest with, begin by asking the Lord to lead you to the right person(s). Go to your pastor and explain to him what you need to do. See if, perhaps, he would be an accountability friend for you, or would recommend someone he knows who can be trusted with such sensitive information. Let your pastor or Christian brother(s) read *chapter 6* of this book so they will have a clear understanding of what you are wanting to accomplish through transparent honesty and accountability. Further professional counseling may be recommended in some instances and is nothing to be afraid of. The main thing to remember is that once you have found a Christian in whom you may confide, it is *vital to maintain* a regular accountability friendship.

IRON SHARPENS IRON

Proverbs 27:17 says:

> *"As iron sharpens iron, a friend sharpens a friend."* (NLT)

How many people can you actually call *friend*? In *Proverbs 27:17,* the word *"friend"* is translated from the original Hebrew word *rea.* The fundamental drift of *rea* is: *a personal companion with whom you can reveal confidences and to whom you sense an extreme nearness.*

To have a true friend with whom you can be transparently honest, and in whom you can trust to give honest feedback is a refreshing fragrance to the soul:

> *"The heartfelt counsel of a friend is as sweet as perfume and incense."*
>
> (Proverbs 27:9 [NLT])

Developing an accountability friendship with at least two people is a development of a friendship in which you can feel safe to share your deepest struggles with sexual temptation, and in which you can expect to be asked "hard questions" of accountability. An example of some of the "hard questions" my accountability friends ask me include:

1. Have you been exposed to any sexually immoral images or indulged in sexual fantasy during the past week?
2. Have you contemplated accessing any form of pornography during the past week?
3. Have you found yourself in a vulnerable situation which could potentially be interpreted as, or lead to inappropriate sexual behavior during the past week?
4. Have you been tempted to act out in any form of sexual immorality during the past week?

You and your accountability friends can formulate questions specifically tailored to your own situation, but the primary thing is to maintain the accountability friendship by meeting with each other *at least* once a week. There may be some weeks when temptations become so intense that you need to contact your accountability friends on a daily basis and acknowledge to them that you are being drawn in the wrong direction by heavy temptation:

> *"You must warn each other every day, as long as it is called 'today', so that none of you will be deceived by sin and hardened against God."*
>
> (Hebrews 3:13 [NLT])

Keep in mind that a good accountability friendship makes room for *constructive criticism.* In other words, if I begin to rationalize or minimize thoughts and behavior which could lead me back in the direction of sexual sin, I need my accountability friends to point it out to me. A true friend should not be afraid to "wound me" with counsel that is for my own benefit. Therefore, be open to constructive criticism as if your life depends upon it—it actually does.

> *"Wounds from a friend are better than many kisses from an enemy."*
>
> (Proverbs 27:6 [NLT])

Maintaining a transparently honest accountability friendship is indeed like iron sharpening iron when it comes to keeping us acute in our thinking toward sexual immorality. The interchange of honest communication with a true friend who wants the highest good for us hones and sharpens us to resist the persistent compulsive preoccupation with sexual immorality. How does this happen? It is via the "exit ramp" of transparent honesty—honesty with yourself, honesty with God, and honesty with another Christian—that the active and operative power of God will *"...keep [sexual] temptation from becoming so strong that you can't stand up against it..."* (1 Corinthians 10:13 [NLT] bracket mine)

THE HIGH POINT OF PRAYER

A jail and prison missionary/evangelist named John Lancaster has been one of my accountability friends. On a recent Wednesday night I met with him and briefly discussed 'where I am' this week concerning my victory over sexual addiction. We culminated our meeting with prayer. I walked away from that meeting to lead a prison worship service with a fresh sense of healing and revival from God's power flowing into my life. Prayer must be the high point of an accountability friendship:

> *"Confess your sins to each other and **pray for each other** so that you may be **healed**.*

> *The earnest prayer of a righteous person has **great power** and **wonderful results**."*
>
> (James 5:16 [NLT])

WHAT ABOUT M - A - S - T - U - R - B - A - T - I - O - N ?

I actually wanted to avoid the entire subject of masturbation. I mean, it is one of those words I almost feel like I need to spell out in a whispering voice if I am discussing it with another Christian, lest someone else hear what I am saying since 'us Christians' certainly don't broach such a subject as m-a-s-t-u-r-b-a-t-i-o-n...shhh...did I write that quietly enough?

Seriously though, the majority of what we do hear about the subject of masturbation tends to be negative in nature, and simply a prohibited act for followers of Christ. I suppose the most obvious reason that masturbation is seen as a negative behavior is the fact that it is most commonly companioned by thoughts of sexually immoral fantasy, which is certainly a sin all by itself. Masturbation also has a tendency to increase in occurrence and become an obsessive habit, especially for the sexual addict. Obviously enslavement to the obsessive pattern of masturbation is a transgression against biblical precept:

> *"You may say, 'I am allowed to do anything.' But I reply, 'Not everything is good for you.' And even though 'I am allowed to do anything,* ***'I must not become a slave to anything."***
>
> (1 Corinthians 6:12 [NLT])

Because masturbation has a tendency to become a compulsive habit, this is an important issue for the sexual addict. Is there *ever* an appropriate time for a Christian to masturbate (especially if you are a recovered sexual addict)? We will answer that question in a moment.

We certainly know that the sex-drive and desire is given to us by God. The natural desire for sexual intimacy is absolutely normal. In fact, there is just no comparable gift so beautiful when sexual intimacy is shared by a Christian husband and wife as they abide in an ever-increasing oneness and love within the sanctum of their marriage bed.

I have met less than five Christians within my lifetime who claim to have the God-given gift of "singleness" (i.e., celibacy). I know there are many more I have not met; however, the majority of Christians do not have the gift of "singleness", rather, they have a God-given sex-drive and desire for marriage.

Christian marriage is the only proper relationship for expressing one's sex-drive and desire through sexual intercourse. The husband and wife are to satisfy and fulfill one another's sexual longings:

> *"The husband should not deprive his wife of sexual intimacy, which is her right as a married woman, nor should the wife deprive her husband. The wife gives authority over her body to her husband, and the husband also gives authority over his body to his wife."*
>
> (1 Corinthians 7:3,4 [NLT])

A healthy sexual intimacy between husband and wife leaves no room for the desire to look elsewhere for sexual fulfillment. Actually, one of the benefits of a healthy sexual intimacy within Christian marriage is the fact that it fends off sexual temptation from outside the marriage. That is the thought when the apostle Paul wrote:

> *"But if they [those who aren't married and widows] can't control themselves, they should go ahead and marry.* ***It's better to marry than to burn with lust."***
>
> (1 Corinthians 7:9 [NLT] brackets mine)

When natural sex-drive and desire does not have an appropriate way of being fulfilled, it can lead to *"burning with lust"*. Even within the healthy Christian marriage, the Word of God warns against prolonged sexual abstinence:

> *"So do not deprive each other of sexual relations. The only exception to this rule would be the agreement of both husband and wife to refrain from sexual intimacy for a* ***limited time****, so they can give themselves more completely to prayer. Afterward they should come together again so* ***that Satan won't be able to tempt them because of their lack of self-control."***
>
> (1 Corinthians 7:5 [NLT])

This verse makes it clear that healthy sexual intimacy within the context of Christian marriage repels Satan's attempts to play on our unfulfilled sex-drive and desires by tempting us.

Having said all of that, it is obvious that within a healthy Christian marriage, the temptation and need is eliminated for husband and wife to satisfy their individual sexual-drive and desires by turning to masturbation apart from each other and the intimacy of "love-making". This leads us back around to our question: *Is there ever an appropriate time for a Christian to masturbate?*

A great number of Christians I know would give an automatic "No!" to that question and change the subject. Nevertheless, let us seriously consider that question with a little bit of grace for just a moment. What if a husband is going through an especially prolonged period of sexual deprivation because his wife is experiencing a serious illness? Does his sex-drive and desire for sexual fulfillment automatically go away because of his wife's illness? Of course not. Could he become more susceptible and vulnerable to sexually immoral temptation because of his extended lack of sexual intimacy? According to *1 Corin-*

thians 7:5 he could. Would it be immoral for this man to use masturbation as a temporary substitute for releasing natural sexual tension so he is not so vulnerable to sexual temptation outside of the marriage? As long as he keeps his thoughts in line with his love for his wife, is masturbation a sin for this man?

What about the Christian husband and wife who experience prolonged times apart because the husband travels a lot with his job? What about the husband and wife who are experiencing long-term portions of time away from each other because one of them is deployed in the military, or one of them is serving a jail/prison sentence, or any number of possible legitimate scenarios which cause extended periods of sexual deprivation? Is masturbation a suitable choice for them to practice as a temporary substitute if they begin to *"burn in their lust"* and feel vulnerable to sexually immoral temptation outside of the marriage? As long as they think about their spouses when they practice the temporary substitute of masturbation, is it a sin for these Christians? What about the unmarried Christian who longs to enter into a God-honoring marriage someday, but in the meantime occasionally uses masturbation as a means of keeping their sex-drive and desires in check to prevent them from entering into sexual intercourse outside of Christian marriage? If they simply go through the motions of masturbation without any accompanying sexually immoral thoughts or fantasy, is it a sin for these unmarried Christians?

These are questions which ultimately have to be answered between these people and God. However, there are highly respected Christian counselors and pastors who concur that the temporary, occasional practice of masturbation is a safe alternative for quenching the fires of burning temptation which we become susceptible to when our natural sex-drive and desire goes unmet, as long as this practice is not accompanied by sexually immoral fantasy.

I have Christians ask me about masturbation quite often and seem to struggle with the guilt of giving in to it (mostly single or divorced men). My response is to explain to them that, ideally, we are to have our natural sexual desires met within the confines of a Christian marriage and would have no need for masturbation. However, if there are circumstances which prevent you from experiencing frequent sexual intimacy with your spouse, or perhaps you are unmarried and want to honor God by abstaining from premarital sexual intercourse, occasional masturbation (**without sexually immoral fantasy**) is a method some people use to prevent the flames of sexually immoral temptation from becoming a blazing inferno of compulsion that will lead you across the line into sexual sin with another person, or any other self-defeating and self-destructive sexual behavior.

I am not promoting masturbation; rather, as a **last resort**, it can be used if absolutely necessary to prevent you from plunging into compulsive sexual sin. However, I must counsel you that it is extremely difficult, if not impossible, to masturbate *without* introducing some degree of sexual mental imagery into your thought processes. Sexually immoral fantasy is a hindrance to the active and operative power of God's Holy Spirit in our lives. Thus, while we may have good intentions for using masturbation as a means for dealing with our "lack of self-control" and "burning with lust", masturbation can actually *increase* our lack of self-control and burning desire if the masturbation is accompanied with any measure of sexually immoral fantasy.

Lack of self-control is really our dilemma, otherwise there would never be a reason for turning to masturbation in the first place. I used *1 Corinthians 7:5* earlier in this section to show you that Satan can utilize prolonged sexual abstinence to tempt Christians into stepping outside the boundaries of marriage and committing sexual sin because of *"...their lack of self-control."* (NLT) However, I would be remiss if I did not explain to you that the apostle Paul was writing to a relatively young church in Corinth. That local church was approximately five years old at the time Paul wrote that letter *(1 Corinthians)* to them.

Corinth was a city of about 500,000 residents from a broad range of social, national, economic, and religious backgrounds. All of the Mediterranean world loved visiting the city of Corinth because it was a place where moral standards did not exist, and thinking was not restrained by deference to any one particular religious belief or philosophy—a city of "free thought". A by-product of Corinth's moral and religious relativism was the pervasiveness of sexual immorality. Male and female prostitution was rampant, and the temple of Aphrodite was a place where "worshipers" could purchase any of the 1,000 temple prostitutes as part of carrying out religious ritual.

It is from this deeply immoral culture that the members of the Corinthian church came. This young church consisted of members who had grown up in that sex-saturated society and were very desensitized toward sexual sin. A lack of "self-control" in the area of sexual immorality was likely a serious weakness for many of these young Christians. Thus, the Holy Spirit (via the apostle Paul's pen) instructed the Corinthian Christians that:

> *"...if they can't control themselves, they should go ahead and marry. It's better to marry than to burn with lust."*
>
> (1 Corinthians 7:9 [NLT])

Furthermore, the Holy Spirit warned married couples in the local church at Corinth to:

> *"...not deprive each other of sexual relations. The only exception to this rule would be the agreement of both husband and wife to refrain from sexual intimacy for a* ***limited time****, so they can give themselves more completely to prayer. Afterward they should come together again so that Satan won't be able to*

> *tempt them* ***because of their lack of self-control.***"
>
> (1 Corinthians 7:5 [NLT])

However, as these Christians in Corinth continued to mature spiritually, a problem with a "lack of self-control" would have become less and less frequent with time if healthy spiritual development was truly taking place.

The same applies to you and me as Christians today. We may have been desensitized toward sexual sin because of the sex-saturated things we have opened our souls up to in the past. As a result, we may have an especially difficult time with a "lack of self-control" when we go through prolonged times of sexual deprivation. Masturbation may seem like the most logical way of dealing with sexual tension which causes us to "burn with lust" when our natural sex-drive and desire does not have an appropriate way of being fulfilled. Nevertheless, as we develop spiritually and mature as Christian men, *self-control* should become more developed in our lives as well.

Self-control is a quality of God's active and operative Holy Spirit in our lives.

> *"But when the Holy Spirit controls our lives, he will produce this kind of fruit in us...* ***self-control...***"
>
> (Galatians 5:22,23 [NLT])

As I mentioned previously, it is practically impossible to engage in masturbation without introducing some degree of sexual mental imagery into your thought processes. Sexually immoral fantasy (as the sin it is) obstructs the work of God's Holy Spirit within us and consequently blocks the production of self-control. A lack of self-control—especially for the sexual addict—can cause masturbation to increase in occurrence and become an obsessing habit.

Therefore, my challenge to you is to abstain from masturbation altogether. You do this by allowing the Holy

Spirit of God to produce a greater intensity of self-control in your life as a maturing Christian man. I will explain how you can do that in the next chapter of this book.

As Christian men, we want to reserve all of our sexual energy for the beautiful intimacy shared by a Christian husband and wife as they abide in ever-increasing oneness and love within the sanctum of their marriage bed. If you are having to wait for that moment and are experiencing a prolonged time of sexual deprivation, I want to remind you:

> *"[Jesus said] My grace is sufficient for thee: for my strength is made perfect in weakness..."*
>
> (2 Corinthians 12:9 [brackets mine])

As we grow in our abiding relationship with Jesus Christ, the Holy Spirit will produce more self-control in our lives, and God's grace will be sufficient for keeping any unmet sexual desires in check. As we exercise self-control and walk in the sufficiency of God's grace, we will no longer have to turn to masturbation. Your sinful nature will try and urge you to give in to masturbation, but you have no obligation to do what your flesh tries to convince you to do:

> *"...you have no obligation whatsoever to do what your sinful nature urges you to do."*
>
> (Romans 8:12 [NLT])

As long as we are walking in God's sufficient grace and allowing His Holy Spirit to produce self-control in our lives, we will have no reason to give in to masturbation, and we can enjoy a new level of sexual purity that is far more gratifying than masturbation could ever be.

If you would like to learn more about how to allow God's Holy Spirit to produce a greater intensity of "self-control" in your life, pay very close attention to the next chapter of this book.

PRACTICAL HOLINESS CHECKLIST

(For Personal Study and Discussion with Accountability Friends)

Practical Application # 1: Be transparently honest with yourself, God, and another Christian about your deepest sexual frailties and weaknesses; then, maintain an accountability friendship.

1. Is the condemning social climate toward sexual offenses preventing you from being transparently honest about a secret struggle with compulsive sexual thoughts and/or behavior?

   It is only when the sexual addict becomes transparently honest with *himself, God,* and *another Christian* that victory over sexual sin, and genuine freedom from shame can be experienced. (see *Proverbs 28:13*)

2. Is the sense of shame associated with sexual addiction causing you to "camouflage" your secret by blending in with the "trees of pretense" so you can hide what is really going on in your life?

   The paradox of it all is that God's enabling power to escape sexual addiction becomes active and operative in our lives when we acknowledge our disabling weaknesses. (see *2 Corinthians 12:9*)

3. Do you realize that when *1 Corinthians 10:13* says: *"...the temptations that come into your life are no different than what others experience"* (NLT), it implies that no matter how far down the scale your sexually immoral leanings may be, they just belong to being human?

   You are not alone in your struggles; there are countless other Christians who deal with the very same compulsions as yourself. There are countless other

Christians who are escaping the besetting sin of sexual addiction...so can you.

4. Do you realize that the *"way of escape"* God most commonly makes available to the Christian who struggles with compulsive sexual behavior is the "exit ramp" of *transparent honesty and accountability*? Are you choosing to avoid the "exit ramp" of transparent honesty and accountability for fear of losing someone's respect?

   You will ultimately experience *increased* respect by others because of the courage and humility you demonstrate in admitting such a struggle.

5. The "exit ramp" of transparent honesty has three levels of honesty:

   Honesty with yourself
   Are you asking yourself the "*Where am I?*" questions of self-examination when it comes to sexually immoral inclinations?

   Honesty with God
   Although various influences and factors may have attributed to your sexual addiction, are you shifting the blame when it comes to being transparently honest with God about your immoral sexual thoughts and/or behavior, or are you accepting responsibility and honestly confessing your sin to God?

   When we are honest with God about our struggles and admit our complete dependence upon His power to give us victory, we are giving Him free reign to search our hearts and motives for deep-rooted sin which only He can bring to our attention before we are led astray.
   (see *Psalm 139:23,24; Psalm 32:1-5*)

Honesty with another Christian

It is extremely vital that you be transparently honest about the exact nature of your deepest sexual frailties and weaknesses. Otherwise, maintaining an accountability friendship with another Christian will be impossible, and you will not experience victory in your battle against sexual addiction.

Find at least two Christian men [Note: If you are a female, seek out two Christian women] who are wise, mature, and solid in their walk with Christ Jesus. Once you have found someone in whom you can confide, it is of the greatest possible importance that you *maintain* a regular accountability friendship with them.

Developing an accountability friendship is the development of a friendship in which you can feel safe to share your deepest struggles with sexual temptation, and in which you can expect to be asked the "hard questions" of accountability *at least* once a week. [Note: refer to *Accountability Meeting Format* on page 125]

Are you willing to allow yourself to receive "wounds" of constructive criticism from your accountability friends if they notice you are rationalizing or minimizing thoughts and behavior which could lead you back in the direction of sexual sin? (see *Proverbs 27:6; Proverbs 27:17*)

Remember, *prayer* must be the high point of any accountability friendship. Are you and your accountability friends making prayer for each other a priority in your weekly meetings? (see *James 5:16*)

'WHERE AM I' QUESTIONS OF SELF-EXAMINATION

Instructions: Make time to review these questions of self-examination on a daily basis as a way to remain transparently honest with yourself and God, enabling the active and operative power of the Holy Spirit to fill you.

1. *"Where Am I"* today when it comes to my thought-life about sex. Are there any corrections in my thinking I need to make right now?
2. *"Where Am I"* today when it comes to specific sexually immoral desires I've had a tendency towards in my past? If those tendencies try to surface today, how am I willing to counterattack? (for example, will I fight them with prayer; reading or meditating on Scripture; fleeing from temptation; contacting my accountability friends; etc.?)
3. *"Where Am I"* today when it comes to guarding my eyes from dwelling on sexually provocative images. Am I committed to practicing the principle of Job 31:1?
4. *"Where Am I"* today with my underlying motives concerning potentially vulnerable situations and/or interactions with others in which I may find myself tempted? Am I maintaining healthy, responsible boundaries?
5. *"Where Am I"* today with my devoted willingness to seek continuous freedom from sexual impurity and addiction? What efforts am I making today to ensure my success? (for example, perhaps I could learn more of what the Bible teaches about sexuality; be an accountability friend for someone else who struggles with sexual addiction; not watch television shows or movies that arouse immoral sexual desires; make time for memorizing some Bible verses; spend an hour in physical exercise while listening to Christian music; read an inspiring book; commit the day to prayer and fasting; etc.)

   [Note: Conclude your self-examination with the following prayer, or one of your own.]

PRAYER

"Father God, I come to you in the authority of Jesus' name and ask you to search my thoughts and point out anything within my thinking you would like to change today.

"Please transform and renew my thinking about sex to line up with your perfect will, pulling down any sexually immoral strongholds which try to influence my spirit, soul, and behavior today.

"Lord, please keep me mindful of the covenant I have made with my eyes according to *Job 31:1.* Bring to my remembrance the vital importance of maintaining healthy and responsible boundaries today if I encounter potentially vulnerable situations and interactions with others in which I may find myself tempted.

"Dear God, today I devote myself to you and the seeking of continuous freedom from sexual impurity and addiction. Please fill me today with the active and operative power of your Holy Spirit. Thank you, Lord. In Jesus' name, Amen"

SUGGESTED ACCOUNTABILITY MEETING FORMAT

Instructions: Meet with an accountability friend *at least* once a week. Include the following:

(a) Open with prayer;

(b) Accountability friend asks you" Questions of Accountability" **(PART A);**

(c) Discuss "Wounds" of Constructive Criticism **(PART B);**

(d) End meeting with "High Point" of prayer **(PART C)**

PART A: QUESTIONS OF ACCOUNTABILITY

1. Have you been exposed to any sexually provocative images or indulged in any sexual fantasy during this past week?
2. Have you contemplated accessing, or do you possess, any form of pornographic material (i.e., any erotic/provocative images) during this past week?
3. Are there any specific sexually immoral desires/temptations which have been especially strong this past week?
4. Have you found yourself in a potentially vulnerable situation which could be interpreted as, or lead to, inappropriate sexual behavior during this past week? Have you been tempted to violate healthy, responsible boundaries?
5. Have you made time to review your "Where Am I" questions of self-examination on a daily basis during this past week?
6. Is there any sin in your heart which needs to be confessed and forsaken?
7. Have you been transparently honest in answering these questions of accountability?

PART B: "WOUNDS" OF CONSTRUCTIVE CRITICISM

At this time, have your accountability friend point out any rationalizing or minimizing thoughts/behavior he may have picked up on as you answered "Questions of Accountability" in PART A.

PART C: "HIGH POINT" OF PRAYER

Both you and your accountability friend should close the meeting with prayer for each other (i.e., he prays for you, you pray for him). Prayer must be the high point of any accountability friendship.

~ Chapter Seven ~

Undivided Allegiance

Practical Application # 2: Maintain an undivided allegiance to the Lord Jesus Christ.

"I pledge allegiance to the flag of the United States of America!"

How many of us have recited that line as part of the Pledge of Allegiance to our country? We take a stand, place our right hand over the heart, focus our eyes on Old Glory, and make a pledge of allegiance. What exactly are we doing when we "pledge"? We are making an assertion, a promise. What exactly are we asserting and promising? Allegiance, loyalty, devotion to our flag and country and all for which she stands.

There is no greater proof of our patriotic promise of loyalty and devotion than the myriad lives which have been willingly sacrificed on battlefields for the defense of this nation's liberty. The giving of one's life leaves no question about allegiance. I am deeply moved with wonderment when contemplating the reality that someone would voluntarily allow their blood spilled so you, I, and all those we know and love can live a life of freedom. Wow!

I guess many of us are a bit complacent about the liberty we experience in this nation because we have never lived in a country without such independence. Our complacency probably desensitizes us a great deal when it comes to truly comprehending and psychologically absorbing the willing sacrifice of one's life so others can live in freedom.

Now I want to take that line of thought and apply it to an eternal level of truth. As previously discussed in chapter five of this book, all of humankind is born into slavery to the penalty, power, and presence of sin. (see *Romans 5:12*) We were doomed to experience an eternal, but very conscious, tormenting separation from God. Eternally! Everlasting! Never-ending! Perpetually!

Someone might say, "That's okay! If I go to hell, I may not ever get to go to heaven, but I'll eventually be annihilated in hell, cease to exist, and will never know the difference forevermore!"

That kind of teaching about hell is called the *doctrine of annihilation.* It is a false teaching that leads people to believe that when a person dies and goes to the torments of hell, ultimately there is a cessation of existence for that person's spirit/soul and he will cease from his suffering and torment. What a *doctrine of devils* that is!

First, it is important to understand that we have souls which are immortal (i.e., made in the image of God). Not even the hottest fires of hell can annihilate the immortal soul of mankind. Someone might say, "Wait a minute John Brown, *Matthew 10:28* tells us to *'...fear only God, who can **destroy** both soul and body in hell.'*"

That is true, but the Greek word translated "destroy" in that verse is the same Greek word translated as "perish" in *Matthew 9:17*:

> *"Neither do men put new wine into old bottles: else the bottles break, and the wine runneth out and bottles **perish**..."*

The fermenting gases of wine built up enough pressure to cause the bottles to burst into pieces. The bottles *did not* cease to exist, rather, their designed purpose was no longer able to be fulfilled. In that sense, they were *destroyed;* in that sense they *perished.* The bottles *still existed* in the form of shattered pieces.

The same applies to the "destruction" or "perishing" of a person's soul in hell. That soul does not cease to exist, rather it is "destroyed" and "perishes" in the sense that it is eternally beyond fulfilling the purpose for which God originally designed it. Hell is eternal! Punishment in hell is eternal! Please, do not allow anyone to sell you the *wind of doctrine* which twists the Scripture in an effort to convince you that a soul will be annihilated in hell and eventually cease to exist.

Second, God never sends anyone to hell at judgment who has not first *chosen* to go to hell. When a person *chooses* to reject the reception of Jesus Christ as Lord and Savior into their life, that person is simultaneously *choosing* hell as their eternal destination:

> *"There is no judgment awaiting those who trust him. But those who do not trust him have already been judged* ***for not believing in the only son of God."***
>
> (John 3:18 [NLT])

> *"...[Jesus] will come with his mighty angels, in flaming fire, bringing judgment on those who don't know God and on those* ***who refuse to obey the Good News of our Lord Jesus****."*
>
> (2 Thessalonians 1:7,8 [NLT] brackets mine)

Why am I telling you all of this bad news about how we humans are born into slavery to the penalty, power, and presence of sin? Why am I telling you that we are doomed to experience an eternal, but very conscious, tormenting separation from God in hell? Well, I'm telling you this bad news so I can get to the good news!

The good news is that mankind does not *have* to spend his life on earth as a slave to the penalty and power of sin! Neither does he *have* to spend an eternity separated from God in a hell of torment!

> *"But God showed his great love for us by sending Christ to die for us while we were still sinners. And since we have been made right in God's sight* ***by the blood of Christ****, he will certainly save us from God's judgment."*
>
> (Romans 5:8,9 [NLT])

Just as men and women have demonstrated their loyalty and devotion by spilling their blood on battlefields to defend the liberty you and I enjoy in this country; likewise, on an eternal level of truth, God demonstrated His undivided allegiance to mankind by becoming a man and voluntarily spilling His divine blood on Calvary's cross so we can enjoy an eternal freedom from slavery to the penalty, power, and eventual presence of sin! Hallelujah! (see *Philippians 2:5-8; Hebrews 2:14*)

The blood spilled for our eternal freedom and privilege to become members of the church of God was the very blood of God Himself:

> *"...the church of God, which he hath purchased with* ***his own blood****."*
>
> (Acts 20:28)

What is the value of just one drop of God's blood? The undivided allegiance He demonstrated toward you and me is priceless. It truly is an amazing grace and mercy that could, perhaps, leave us in an eternal state of wonderment.

OUR REASONABLE SERVICE

If Christ Jesus freely spilled His blood and died as the sacrifice for you and me on Calvary's cross so we could live a life of freedom from sin's control, it is only reasonable that we *die to self* and live a sacrificial life in allegiance to our Savior:

> *"I beseech you therefore, brethren, by the mercies of God, that ye present your bodies a*

living sacrifice, holy, acceptable unto God, which is ***your reasonable service."***

(Romans 12:1)

God willingly yielded His life for you and me on that old rugged cross. It is only *reasonable* (i.e., logical) that we *yield* (i.e., sacrifice) our lives for Him on a daily basis by demonstrating our undivided allegiance to Jesus in all areas of our lives.

When *Romans 12:1* says we are to *"present [our] bodies"*, it is referring to every fiber of my being as *spirit, soul, body.* I am to offer my selfless, undivided loyalty to Christ Jesus out of love and appreciation for the selfless, undivided allegiance He offered for me at the cross:

"We love him, because he first loved us."

(1 John 4:19)

BANANAS!

One of the advantages of our undivided allegiance to the Lord Jesus Christ is the *fruit of His Spirit* in our lives. The more active and operative I allow God's Holy Spirit to be in my life, the more intense are the qualities of the fruit of the Spirit, and less likely are my fleshly impulses to gain a stronghold over my mind and behavior. Conversely, the more I *grieve* and *quench* the active and operative ministry of the Holy Spirit in my life, the more obstructed are the qualities of the fruit of the Spirit, and greater the danger of my fleshly impulses gaining a stronghold over my mind and behavior.

We know that nine qualities of the fruit of God's Holy Spirit are listed in *Galatians 5:22,23*:

"But when the Holy Spirit controls our lives, he will produce this kind of fruit in us: love, joy, peace, patience, kindness, goodness, faithfulness, gentleness, and self-control..."

(NLT)

As someone who has been delivered from sexual addiction, the development of *all* these qualities in my life is important to my continued victory over sexual immorality. However, I especially take note of "**self-control**". In this verse, "*self-control"* is translated from the original Greek word which means: *the quality of a person who has mastered his lusts and passions, especially when it comes to sexual appetites.*

The spiritual fruit of self-control is not produced by you or me; it is *only* produced by the active and operative Holy Spirit of God through our lives. Now any of us can certainly "manufacture" what may appear to be genuine fruit of the Spirit. We can act all religious and do all the sanctimonious religious stuff, say all the religious words and appear to bear the fruit of God's Holy Spirit in our lives when, in reality, underneath our religious facade we are hollow and empty of the active and operative power of God in our lives.

When I was about three years old I spent many of my days at Mamaw and Papaw Morphew's home while my parents worked. Mamaw always had fresh fruit available for me to snack on. I loved the bananas, I guess, better than anything else.

One day while Mamaw was in the living room, I made my way to the kitchen. I spotted a wooden bowl full of fruit sitting on the center of the table. It was filled with shiny red apples, juicy looking oranges, plump purple grapes and, yes, bananas!

I climbed up on one of the dining chairs and reached across the table for a delicious banana. As soon as I had the banana in my hand I knew something about it was odd. It looked very appetizing, but it felt different. It was an unusual texture...didn't weigh much...and it was...plastic!

I had in my hand an artificial banana that was manufactured to appear real, but it was just a plastic, hollow, empty piece of *artificial* fruit.

Let me tell you from experience, we can be as "religious" as we want to be and try to manufacture the fruit of God's Spirit in our own power, but when we are faced with the overpowering compulsion of sexual temptation, if the fruit of *self-control* is not the genuine fruit of God's active and operative Holy Spirit, we have no defense against compulsive sexual behavior. How do we make sure the fruit of *self-control* is the genuine fruit of God's active and operative Holy Spirit? Read on.

ABIDING IN CHRIST

We must move beyond mere ritualistic, shallow, hollow, empty religiosity. We must move into the intimate, personal love relationship Christ Jesus desires to have with us. This is the *only* way His Spirit will actively and operatively produce the fruit of *self-control* in our lives so we can consistently live victoriously over sexual addiction.

The Bible teaches us in Christ's own words:

> *"I am the vine, ye are the branches:* ***He that abideth in me****, and I in him, the same* ***bringeth forth much fruit****: for without me ye can do nothing."*
>
> (John 15:5)

This verse tells us several things:

1. Who Christ is: *"I am the vine"*
   He is the nurturing vine.
2. Who we Christians are: *"Ye are the branches"*
   We are the branches connected to the nurturing vine.
3. Our responsibility as Christians: *"He that abideth in me"*
   We are responsible for staying connected (i.e., remaining in our proper and expected relationship) with the nurturing vine.
4. Christ's responsibility to the Christian: *"And I [abideth] in him"*
   Christ *never* fails to be responsible when it comes to remaining in His proper and expected relationship with the branches who depend on His nourishment

(we, the "branches", are the ones who fail to stay connected to Jesus the "vine".)

5. The result of upholding our responsibility of abiding: *"The same bringeth forth much fruit"*

   Much fruit of the Holy Spirit will be produced in our lives if we remain in our proper and expected relationship with Jesus (this includes the quality of "self control".)

6. The result of not upholding our responsibility: *"For without me ye can do nothing"*

   We will be spiritually "fruitless" and powerless as Christians if we fail to remain in our proper and expected relationship with Jesus Christ.

Christ will always have a heart of undivided and abiding allegiance toward the Christian; He proved that on the cross. He is like a faithful bridegroom who never even considered infidelity against His bride. We, on the other hand, have a tendency to get out of our proper and expected relationship with Christ Jesus. We are more like the bride who has an adulterous affair going on behind closed doors.

When our allegiance to Christ is divided with a love affair for things which take precedence over God's will, and when we are not "abiding" in Christ because we have allowed some area of our life to get out of proper and expected relationship with our Lord and Savior, we are guilty of *spiritual adultery:*

> *"You adulterers! Don't you realize that friendship with this world makes you an enemy of God? I say it again, that if your aim is to enjoy this world, you can't be a friend of God. What do you think the Scriptures mean when they say that the Holy Spirit, whom God has placed within us, jealously longs for us to be faithful?"*
>
> (James 4:4,5 [NLT])

Notice those words, "*the Holy Spirit, whom God has placed within us, jealously longs for us to be faithful.*" How are we to be *faithful*? We do it by "abiding" in Jesus Christ. "Abiding", as stated previously, simply means *to remain in our proper and expected relationship*. It is not proper or expected for a bride or groom to have an adulterous relationship with someone else. The bride and groom are to *abide* within the *oneness* of their union.

Likewise, Christians have entered into a type of marriage [oneness] with Jesus Christ:

> "*...Ye also are become dead to the law by the body of Christ; that ye should be* ***married*** *to another, even to him who is raised from the dead,* ***that we should bring forth fruit unto God.***"
>
> (Romans 7:4)

This verse shows us that the natural result of our *marriage* to Christ is"*...that we should bring forth fruit unto God.*" Thus, if I am remaining in my proper and expected relationship with Christ Jesus, the genuine and abundant fruit of God's Holy Spirit will be birthed in and through my life. This Holy Spirit fruit includes *self-control* for mastering the lusts and passions associated with sexual addiction.

The problem often lies in the fact that many of us Christians have grown complacent by failing to remain wholehearted in our abiding relationship with Christ. Consequently, any part of our heart that is having a love affair with worldliness (i.e., the worldly system that mankind has constructed to satisfy his fleshly appetites which take precedence over God's will) is a part of our heart in which we have built an "idol" and *limited* the spiritual fruit of God in our lives:

> "*...they turned back and tempted God, and* ***limited*** *the Holy One of Israel.*"
>
> (Psalm 78:41)

GOLDEN CALVES AND ALTARS TO GOD

Let us revisit the historical record of the Israelites as they camped at the base of Mount Sinai following their deliverance from Egyptian slavery. We pick up the event at *Exodus 24:12* where God tells Moses to climb the mountain and receive the stone tablets with God's instructions which Moses was to use in teaching the two million or so Israelites.

As we read in the biblical record we learn that Joshua accompanied Moses part of the way up Mount Sinai while Aaron and Hur were left in charge of the Israelites camped at the foot of the mountain.

Moses and Joshua apparently set up a camp for themselves part of the way up the mountain for six days as the glory cloud of the LORD formed at the top of the mountain. On the seventh day God called to Moses from out of the cloud. Moses left Joshua and climbed onward toward the apex of Mount Sinai and entered the midst of God's glory. *Exodus 24:18* tells us that Moses was on the mountain forty days and forty nights.

While this was going on, the Israelites were able to observe an incredibly impressive occurrence from their perspective at the foot of Mount Sinai. Can you envision what they saw while looking skyward almost 8,000 feet at the peak of that mountain?

> *"The Israelites at the foot of the mountain saw an awesome sight. The awesome glory of the LORD on the mountaintop looked like a devouring fire."*
>
> (Exodus 24:17 [NLT])

We now scan forward to *Exodus 32.* It had been almost forty days since Moses went to the top of Mount Sinai. The Israelites were beginning to think that surely Moses had disappeared and was not coming back:

> *"When Moses failed to come back down the mountain right away, the people went to Aaron. 'Look', they said, 'make us some gods*

who can lead us. This man Moses, who brought us here from Egypt, has disappeared. We don't know what has happened to him.' "

(Exodus 32:1 [NLT])

Upon hearing such a request, this would have been the appropriate time for Aaron to remind the Israelites of the commandments which had been orally delivered to them back in *chapter 20*—most specifically:

"I am the LORD your God, who rescued you from slavery in Egypt. Do not worship any other gods besides me. Do not make idols of any kind, whether in the shape of birds or animals or fish. You must never worship or bow down to them, for I, the LORD your God, am a jealous God who will not share your affection with any other god!..."

(Exodus 20:2-5 [NLT])

Well, Aaron failed to put his sandal-clad foot down on this issue. Instead, he went along with the idolatry by collecting all of Israel's gold earrings and melting the gold, molding it and using a graving tool to shape it into the image of a calf. Then Aaron said to the Israelites:

"...These be thy gods, O Israel, which brought thee up out of the land of Egypt."

(Exodus 32:4)

That is just mind-boggling to me! The Israelites reverted back to the worship they had been accustomed to observing the Egyptians practice for so many centuries. There seemed to always be a natural bent for the Israelites to revert back to their "comfort zone" of Egyptian slavery when it actually was a "zone of bondage".

What's more mind-boggling to me is what happened next:

> *"When Aaron saw how excited the people were about it [the golden calf], **he built an altar** in front of the calf and announced, 'Tomorrow there will be a festival **to the Lord!'** So the people got up early the next morning to sacrifice burnt offerings and peace offerings. After this, they celebrated with feasting and drinking, and indulged themselves in pagan revelry."*
>
> (Exodus 32:5,6 [NLT] brackets mine)

This is the perfect picture of a *divided allegiance* to God. Right in front of this pagan idol, Aaron erected "*an altar...to the Lord!*" The next day they performed their "religious ritual" to God on the altar, then they partied hearty and indulged in full-throttle immorality centered around the gold calf idol. The Israelites were certainly not remaining in their proper and expected relationship with God by doing this. They were actually involved in *spiritual adultery.*

WHO IS ON THE LORD'S SIDE? LET HIM COME UNTO ME!

We read in *Exodus 32:7* that the Lord told Moses to quickly move down the mountain and confront the Israelites because they had turned from the way God had commanded them to live. In fact, God was ready to destroy them. Moses pleaded with God to hold back His wrath and give the Israelites another chance.

When Moses got near the base of the mountain, Joshua was waiting on him. When they arrived at the base camp, Moses was angered and threw the covenant-inscribed stone tablets to the ground, shattering them to pieces. (This was a display of what the Israelites had already done to their covenant with God in their hearts.) Moses then took the golden calf, burned it, ground it into a powder, mixed it with water and made the Israelites drink it. (Spiritual adultery may taste of sweet pleasure and excitement for a season, but it eventually leads to the repulsive taste of a dirty ashtray when all is said and done.)

Many of the Israelites continued on in their unbridled revelry. That is when Moses shouted:

> *"...Who is on the LORD's side? let him come unto me..."*
>
> (Exodus 32:26)

The first to respond was the tribe of Levi. As a result, the Levites were commanded to strap up with swords and kill any other Israelites who continued in rebellion; even if it was a brother, friend or neighbor. About three thousand people were killed that day because of their spiritual adultery. Following this unfortunate slaughter, in Exodus 32:29 Moses spoke to the Levites and said:

> *"...**Consecrate yourselves** today to the LORD, even every man upon his son, and upon his brother; that he may bestow upon you a blessing this day."*

The undivided allegiance of the Levites is likely why they were chosen to be the "priestly" tribe. They were told to *"consecrate"* themselves today to the LORD. In other words, they were being ordained for a special service of the LORD.

We can so easily do the very same thing the Israelites did when it comes to spiritual adultery. We, as Christians who struggle with sexual addiction, have entered into a covenant (e.g. marriage) with God through the blood of Christ Jesus. We know He loves us so extremely much that He shed His blood for our eternal freedom from slavery to sin. We know that by remaining in our proper and expected relation with Him (i.e., abiding), His Holy Spirit manifests an active and operative power through our lives in the form of spiritual fruit—including the greatly needed fruit of *"self-control"* which gives us victory over compulsive sexual behavior.

We know that it is only reasonable to give our wholehearted, undivided allegiance to Christ Jesus in light of the fact that He has demonstrated His undivided loyalty, love and devotion to us on Calvary's tree. Yet, how many of us have a natural bent for reverting back to our worldly "comfort zones" which are in all reality a "zone of bondage" for us? How many of us have golden calves erected in our hearts right next to our altar to God? How many of us perform our ritualistic religious duties on the "altar of God" by attending church, giving tithes and offerings, singing in the choir, reading our Bible, talking about Jesus, praying, etc... while *at the same time* we have a love affair going on with the "golden calf" of worldliness that mankind has constructed to satisfy our fleshly appetites which take precedence over God's will?

We have to be *honest* about the "idols" in our lives which divide our wholehearted allegiance to Jesus Christ. Some questions we might consider:

1. Does the entertainment in which I indulge (i.e., music, literature, film, Internet, etc.) cater more to the satisfaction and enlargement of my ungodly appetites or God-honoring appetites?

2. Do the friendships and other relationships I have promote God-honoring thoughts, words, and behavior; or, ungodly thoughts, words, behavior?

3. Does my vocation, the love of money and material prosperity take precedence over God's plan and purpose for my life?

4. Do I easily find reasons to skip church services, fellowship and activities in order to "do my own thing"?

5. Do I fail to make quality time in one-to-one communication with the Lord through daily prayer and Bible study?

6. Is there any interest in my life which takes predominance over my commitment to Jesus Christ?

He is asking us the same question each day that Moses asked the spiritually adulterous Israelites:

> *"...Who is on the LORD's side? let him come unto me."*
>
> (Exodus 32:26)

We are to come unto Him daily through abiding—remaining in our proper and expected relationship with Christ Jesus our "Bridegroom"—so the genuine fruit of His Holy Spirit can manifest His powerful qualities into our lives.

This "abiding" relationship is what the Word of God is referring to when it instructs:

> *"Draw nigh to God, and he will draw nigh to you..."*
>
> (James 4:8)

We are to identify the external things of worldliness in which our "hands" should not be involved:

> *"...Cleanse your hands, ye sinners..."*
>
> (James 4:8)

We are also to identify the divided loyalties within our hearts lest we be double-minded like the Israelites with their "golden calf" and "altar of God":

> *"...purify your hearts, ye double-minded"*
>
> (James 4:8)

CONSECRATE YOURSELVES TODAY

As we get closer to wrapping up this chapter of the book, I want to touch on one more thing of importance when it comes to maintaining an undivided allegiance to the Lord Jesus Christ. I want to talk a little bit about *consecration* and how it applies to us as Christians.

We read where the Levites were told to consecrate themselves because they were being ordained for the service of priesthood. (see *Exodus 32:29*) It is good to understand that the word "consecrate" is translated from a Hebrew word which has a twofold import:

1. As part of the priesthood, the Levites were "**set apart"** for the special service of offering sacrifices to God; and,
2. They were also **"given the authority"** to fully represent the special service of priesthood in their daily lives.

   Of course the priesthood under Mosaic Law was limited to the Levites and is no longer operative today; rather, *all* Christians are priests who have automatic access to God through our High Priest Jesus Christ. Praise God! Along with this wonderful blessing of priesthood, we too are called to consecration in a twofold manner:

   a. 1 Peter 2:5 says we are a "**Holy** Priesthood". That means we have been "set apart" for the special service of offering *"spiritual sacrifices".* One of the greatest spiritual sacrifices we can offer up to God is that of a living sacrifice for Him through our wholehearted allegiance to Jesus Christ.

   b. 1 Peter 2:9 says we are a "**Royal** Priesthood". That means we have been given "full authority" to represent the priesthood of Jesus Christ in our daily lives. One of the greatest privileges we have is to be a living representative of Jesus Christ to a lost world, pleading with them that they be reconciled to God:

      > *"We are Christ's ambassadors, and God is using us to speak to you. We urge you, as though Christ himself were here pleading with you, 'Be reconciled to God!' "*
      >
      > (2 Corinthians 5:20 [NLT])

If we take our daily consecration to God as ***Holy*** and ***Royal*** priests more seriously, we will be apt to stay mindful about maintaining an undivided allegiance to the Lord Jesus Christ, and representing Him in all areas of our life. The result, of course, is that we will bring forth much fruit of the Holy Spirit—especially the fruit of *self-control* —to equip us for escaping the besetting sin of sexual addiction.

Remember, it is only by remaining in our proper and expected relationship with Christ Jesus that the active and operative power of God's Holy Spirit can produce the genuine fruit of self-control when it comes to mastering our lusts and passions related to sexual addiction:

> *"For the LORD sees clearly what a man does, examining every path he takes. An evil man is held captive by his own sins; they are ropes that catch and hold him. He will die for* ***lack of self-control****; he will be lost because of his incredible folly."*
>
> (Proverbs 5:21-23 [NLT])

> *"Little children, keep yourselves from idols. Amen."*
>
> (1 John 5:21)

PRACTICAL HOLINESS CHECKLIST

(For Personal Study and Discussion with Accountability Friends)

Practical Application # 2: Maintain an undivided allegiance to the Lord Jesus Christ.

1. Do I truly understand that it is only *reasonable* that I yield my life to God on a daily basis by demonstrating undivided allegiance to Jesus Christ in *all* areas of my life?

    You are to offer your selfless, undivided allegiance to Christ Jesus out of love and appreciation for the selfless, undivided allegiance He offered for you on the cross.
    (see *1 John 4:19; Romans12:1,2*)

2. Am I guilty of practicing a ritualistic, shallow, hollow, empty religiosity which requires me to manufacture realistic looking *artificial* fruit of God's Holy Spirit in my life?

    When you are faced with the overpowering compulsions of sexual temptation, if the fruit of "self-control" is not the *genuine* fruit of God's active and operative Holy Spirit, you will have no defense against compulsive sexual behavior.

    You must move into the undivided, intimate and personal *relationship* Christ Jesus desires to have with you. This is the only kind of relationship which makes a way for the Holy Spirit to produce the spiritual fruit in your life for consistent victory over sexual temptation.
    (see *Galatians 5:16-23; John 15:5*)

3. Am I remaining in my proper and expected relationship with Jesus Christ (i.e., abiding in Him) in *all* areas of my life?

When your allegiance to Christ is divided with a love for things which take precedence over God's will; when you have allowed some area of your life to get out of proper and expected relationship with your Lord and Savior, you are guilty of *spiritual adultery.*

As a Christian, you have entered into a marriage [oneness] with Jesus Christ. When you remain faithful to your union with Him, the genuine and abundant fruit of God's Holy Spirit will be birthed in and through your life, including the fruit of "self-control" for mastering the lusts and passions associated with compulsive sexual behavior.
(see *James 4:4,5; Romans 7:4*)

4. Do I have a natural tendency for retrogressing toward my "comfort zone" of worldliness which is really a "zone of bondage" for me?

Any part of your heart that is having a love affair with worldliness (i.e., the world-system that mankind has constructed to satisfy his appetites outside God's will) is a part of your heart in which you have built an "idol" and have *limited* the active and operative fruit of God's Holy Spirit in your life.
(see *Psalm 78:41*)

5. Am I being honest about the "idols" in my life which divide my wholehearted allegiance to the Lord Jesus Christ?

Some questions of self-examination you might consider:

Does the entertainment in which I indulge cater more to the satisfaction and enlargement of my ungodly appetites or God-honoring appetites?

Do the friendships and relationships I have promote God-honoring thoughts, words, and behavior; or, ungodly thoughts, words, and behavior?

Do my vocation, the love of money and material prosperity take precedence over God's plan and purpose for my life?

Do I easily find reasons to skip church services, fellowship and activities with other Christians in order to "do my own thing"?

Do I fail to *make* quality time in one-to-one communion with the Lord through daily prayer and Bible study?

Is there *any* interest in my life which takes predominance over my commitment to the Lord Jesus Christ?

6. Am I willing to hear God's voice, every day I wake up in this world, as He asks my heart: "*...Who is on the LORD'S side? let him come unto me...?"*

If you draw near to God He promises to draw near to you.

Put a note with the words "*Who is on the Lord's side? let him come unto me"* somewhere that you will see it each morning you awake. Let it be a reminder that when you draw near to God you should:

Identify and let go of the *external* things of worldliness in which your "hands" should not be involved as a Christian; and,

Identify and cut off the *internal* things within your heart which divide your loyalty to Christ and lead you into double-mindedness like the Israelites with their "golden calf" and "altar to God".
(see *Exodus 32:26; James 4:8*)

7. As a *holy* and *royal* priest, do I take seriously my daily consecration to God?

As a *holy* priest, you are **set apart** for the special service of offering *"spiritual sacrifices"*.

One of the greatest spiritual sacrifices you can offer to God is that of being a "living sacrifice" for

Him through your undivided allegiance to Jesus Christ.
(see *1 Peter 2:5; Romans 12:1,2*)

As a *royal* priest, you have been **given the authority** to fully represent your High Priest Jesus Christ in your daily life.

One of the greatest privileges you have is to be a living representative of Jesus Christ for a lost world, pleading that they be reconciled to God.
(see *1 Peter 2:9; 2 Corinthians 5:20*)

~ Chapter Eight ~
Guarding Your Mind

Practical Application # 3: Guard your mind above all else.

I need to begin the chapter by making a distinction between the *brain* and the *mind.* These words are often used synonymously (and rightly so) within certain contexts. However, spiritually speaking, there is a major difference between the brain and the mind.

The brain (and central nervous system as a whole) is so amazingly complex that, within the field of biological study alone, the probability of our brain originating by random evolutionary chance is diminished and brings rise to the greater probability of the Master Designer—God. In fact, all of creation speaks of a Creator. It has been anonymously said: "Within the breast of nature throbs the heart of God."

Praise the Lord!

I just want you to understand that while the *brain* deals with the material and physical facet of mankind's function, the *mind* deals with the immaterial and spiritual facet of mankind's function—primarily speaking: *the soul.* God reveals to us in the Bible that we are threefold in our being:

> *"And the very God of peace sanctify you wholly; and I pray God your whole* ***spirit*** *and* ***soul*** *and* ***body*** *be preserved blameless unto the coming of our Lord Jesus Christ."*
>
> (1 Thessalonians 5:23)

As whole human beings we are *spirit, soul, body:*

1. SPIRIT

The immortal, immaterial portion of our human composition which is interwoven with, and inseparable from, the human soul. The spirit serves as the conduit/filter through which spiritual intake is fed to the soul.

When a person receives Jesus Christ as Lord and Savior, the Holy Spirit of God becomes one with the human spirit as communion with God is activated.

"The [Holy]Spirit itself beareth witness with our [human] spirit, that we are the children of God."

(Romans 8:16 [brackets mine])

"And God has given us his Spirit as proof that we live in him and he in us."

(1 John 4:13 [NLT])

2. SOUL

The immortal, immaterial portion of our human composition which is interwoven with, and inseparable from the human spirit. The human soul is the life force which animates the physical body. The soul is the base of operation for our spiritual intellect (i.e., *spiritual mind*), emotions, self-awareness, and freedom of choice. Our soul is to be progressively transformed into the *mind of Christlikeness.* The soul is also *who* we truly are as individual beings and personalities.

The human soul is that part of us which needs atonement by the blood of Jesus Christ in order to enter God's eternal presence following the death of our physical body.

"...for it is the blood that maketh an atonement ***for the soul****."*

(Leviticus 17:11)

"Your reward for trusting him will be the ***salvation of your souls."***

(1 Peter 1:9 [NLT])

3. BODY
The mortal, physical portion of our human composition which is animated by the life force of our immortal spirit and soul. The human body is a temporary and miraculously designed biological housing for our spirit and soul.

Although the human body will die, *every* human soul will eventually have another body in his eternal destination of heaven or hell.

"Don't be so surprised! Indeed, the time is coming when all the dead in their graves will hear the voice of God's Son, and they will rise again. Those who have done good will rise to eternal life, and those who have continued in evil will rise to judgment."

(John 5:28,29 [NLT])
(also see 1 Corinthians 15)

AN ORDER OF OPERATION

It is no mistake that *1 Thessalonians 5:23* lists our threefold being in the order of *spirit, soul, body.* If you were to ask a number of people to enumerate the threefold composition of our being, a lot of those folks would say we are ***body,*** *soul, spirit,* or ***body,*** *spirit, soul,* or some combination beginning with the word *body.*

The reason we tend to list "body" first is because, subconsciously, we have an established partiality as humans to place priority on the physical realm in which we live. We are more given to put the highest importance on satisfying our "bodily" appetites rather than spirit and soul.

I, myself, am quoted from 1998 in a textbook on alcoholism recovery as saying we are *"...**body,** spirit, soul."* It wasn't until several years later that I understood the divinely-designed order of our composition: spirit, soul, body.

Our *spirit* serves as the conduit/filter through which spiritual intake is fed to the *soul.* The spiritual intake is going to be either godly or ungodly in nature, depending on what kind of spiritual "food" you are feasting. For instance, listening to music which promotes thinking and conduct that is *contrary* to biblical precepts would be considered as *ungodly* spiritual intake. Whereas, listening to music which promotes thinking and conduct that is in harmony with biblical precepts would be considered as *godly* spiritual intake.

[Note: I use music as one example because I worked in the secular music broadcasting industry for numerous years and have witnessed firsthand the vigorous and forceful ungodly influences certain music can have on a person's thinking and behavior. I am not inferring that all music is ungodly if it does not involve religious matters. However, some music is definitely driven by ungodly influences which are detrimental to one's soul.]

It is extremely important to "feed" on *godly spiritual intake* because the things we allow into our *spirit* go directly to our *soul* (i.e., spiritual mind). The condition of my soul/spiritual mind influences my bodily/external choices and behavior.

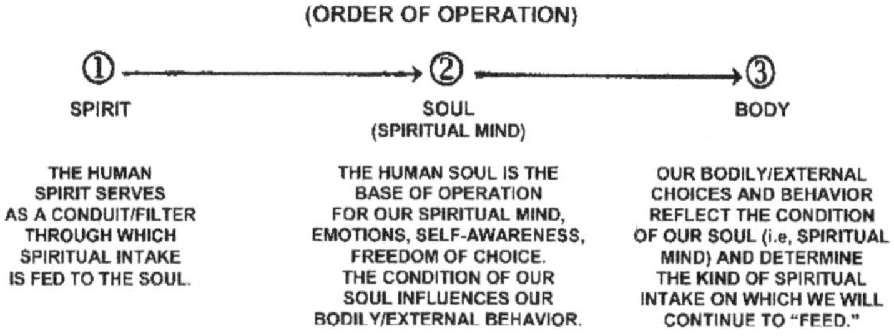

The condition of my *soul* (i.e., spiritual mind) is very noticeably important since it determines the bodily/external choices and behavior I manifest through my *body*. Why is it so important for the sexual addict to understand this truth? Because if we are deliberate enough in allowing our *spirit* to feed on godly spiritual intake, then our *soul* will continue developing in a Christlike condition. The Christlike condition of my soul will be reflected in sexually pure physical/external choices and behavior with my *body*.

YOUR SPIRITUAL FILTER

You've probably heard of an Internet filter. Those are great to have on your computer because they filter out any "impure" materials that they are instructed to reject before making it to your monitor.

You've heard of water filters. Those, too, are great to have because they remove the impurities from your water before you drink it.

As mentioned previously, your human spirit serves as a filter through which spiritual intake is fed to your soul/spiritual mind. The only way that I am going to protect my spiritual mind from the impure spiritual intake which wants to corrupt it, is to reject that impure intake from getting past my spirit in the first place. Just like an Internet or water filter, I must stop the impurities dead in their tracks as soon as they try getting beyond my spirit into the more advanced point of my soul where the "impurities" assemble strongholds within my spiritual mind.

HAVE YOU LOST YOUR MIND?

In a military battle you might hear that a certain city was "lost" to a conquering army. What that means is that the conquering army acquired victory over the city by force of warfare and caused the previous inhabitants to "lose" dominion of the city.

If you will, think of your soul/spiritual mind as a city. Your greatest enemies are the *devil,* your *sinful nature,* and *worldliness.* I once heard Dr. David Jeremiah preach a sermon over the radio about these three enemies of our soul. He said we need to *fight* the devil, *flee* the sinful nature, and *forsake* worldliness. I like that. Yes, we need to *fight, flee,* and *forsake* the attempts of our enemies when they want to gain victory over the "city" of our soul/spiritual mind.

> *"Above all else, **guard** your heart [mind], for it affects everything you do."*
>
> (Proverbs 4:23, [NLT] brackets mine)

Remember, the condition of your "spiritual mind" *...affects everything you do* when it comes to your bodily/external choices and behavior. Thus, we must ***guard*** our mind. Also notice that the verse says: *"Above all else..."* That emphasizes the priority of persistent personal attention we are to give to the guarding of our mind.

I do not want to "lose" my spiritual mind to the conquering armies of *Satan, my sinful nature,* and *worldliness.* As a recovered sexual addict, a loss of my spiritual mind to the influences of these enemies means further compulsive sexual behavior and the ruinous consequences which are sure to ensue.

We must *never* forget there is a very real spiritual war going on against our mind:

> *"For I delight in the law of God after the inward man: But I see another law in my members, **warring against** the law of **my mind**, and bringing me into captivity to the law of sin which is in my members."*
>
> (Romans 7:22,23)

> *"Dearly beloved, I beseech you as strangers and pilgrims, abstain from fleshly lusts, which **war against the soul**."*
>
> (1 Peter 2:11)

The term *"war against"* means that an enemy encampment is setting up a "base of operation" closer, and closer, and closer to your soul/spiritual mind in an effort to conquer. Our only hope against these spiritual enemies is to stop giving them ground!

BUILDING A WALL WITH TOWERS

Many ancient cities had walls built around the entire city, essentially becoming a citadel against attack. The city also had towers built at various intervals atop the walls. Those towers were to be manned by watchmen defending the city against attack.

Likewise, we must have a *boundary wall* around our soul/spiritual mind to define what things can and cannot enter. Then we must build *towers* atop the walls that will serve as a defense against enemy attack.

Boundary Walls. Let us first consider the boundary walls. The Word of God says:

> *"He that hath no rule over his own spirit is like a city that is broken down, and without walls."*
>
> (Proverbs 25:28)

If we fail to establish a *boundary wall* within our spirit that defines and limits the kind of spiritual intake allowed to enter, our soul/spiritual mind will become like an undefended city which is open to any method of attack. This has so often been the case for the Christian who struggles with sexual addiction: *Sexual temptation presents the lure; the addict takes the bait as compulsive preoccupation is incited within the mind; the addict then manifests sexually immoral action through his bodily/external choices and behavior; as a result, death is produced in the sexual addict's life.*

I can hear someone saying, "Wait a minute, John Brown, what do you mean *death* is produced?" Let's look at James 1:14,15—

> *"But every man is tempted, when he is drawn away of his own lust, and enticed. Then when lust hath conceived, it bringeth forth sin: and sin, when it is finished, bringeth forth* ***death****."*

For the Christian sexual addict, this does not mean that he experiences spiritual death by losing his salvation when giving in to sexual temptation. Nor does it mean that he experiences physical death (although sexual sin often causes physical death by virus, disease, etc.). What this verse does mean for the Christian sexual addict is that he will experience a kind of "living death" by way of ruptured and broken communion with the Spirit of God. An example of this can be found in reference to the Christian widow who chose to live in a backslidden state of sinful pleasure:

> *"But she that liveth in pleasure is* ***dead while she liveth."***
>
> (1 Timothy 5:6)

She did not lose her salvation, but because of her choice to live in sinful pleasure, she is experiencing a kind of "living death" as far as her communion with God's Holy Spirit and His designed purpose for her life are concerned.

Most Christian sexual addicts have experienced this funereal type of "living death" on multiple occasions. It is a grim and darkening place to be. How do we prevent ourselves from plunging to such depths of misery and hopelessness? Well, in part, when sexual temptation presents the lure, we must stop taking the bait. We do this by building a *boundary wall* within our spirit that defines and limits the kind of spiritual intake allowed to enter.

Our boundary walls must be constructed with the "brick" and "mortar" of the inspired and infallible Word of God. The *Bible* is the "brick" we are to use in constructing our walls. *Obedience* to the Bible is the "mortar" which holds our walls together. Jesus teaches:

> *"Whosoever cometh to me, and* ***heareth*** *my sayings [word] and* ***doeth*** *them, I will show you to whom he is like: He is like a man which built a house, and digged deep, and laid the foundation on a rock: and when the flood arose, the storm beat vehemently upon*

> *that house, and could not shake it: for it was founded upon a rock."*
>
> (Luke 6:47-48 [brackets mine])

> *"But be ye doers of the word, and not hearers only, deceiving your own selves."*
>
> (James 1:22)

The Word of God is spiritually alive and powerful (see *Hebrews 4:12*). God's word teaches us the proper boundaries we need in order to maintain victorious lives over sin:

> *"All Scripture is inspired by God and is useful to teach us what is true and to make us realize what is wrong in our lives. It straightens us out and teaches us to do what is right. It is God's way of preparing us in every way, fully equipped for every good thing God wants us to do."*
>
> (2 Timothy 3:16,17 [NLT])

> *"Thy word have I hid in mine heart, that I might not sin against thee."*
>
> (Psalm 119:11)

The Word of God is alive enough and powerful enough to penetrate and engrave itself into the innermost merging point of the spirit and soul. That is where your boundary walls must be constructed:

> *"For the word of God is quick, and powerful, and sharper than any two-edged sword, piercing even to the dividing asunder of soul and spirit..."*
>
> (Hebrews 4:12)

Furthermore, the Word of God is an accurate filter for safeguarding your mind:

"For the word of God is ...a discerner of the thoughts and intents of the heart."

(Hebrews 4:12)

When our spiritual diet includes a **daily** intake of God's Word, *and* obedience to His Word, we are constructing a solid *boundary wall* within our spirit that defines and limits the kind of spiritual intake allowed to enter our soul/mind.

Towers. Now let us consider the towers we need to construct atop our boundary walls. The Word of God says:

"The watchman on the tower of Jezreel saw Jehu and his company approaching, so he shouted to Joram, 'I see a company of troops coming!'"

(2 Kings 9:17 [NLT])

Our *towers* should serve as guardhouses which keep us alert to the potential dangers of temptation which threaten our sexual purity. We must determine what "towers" we need, based on our own individual struggles. For example some of my towers include:

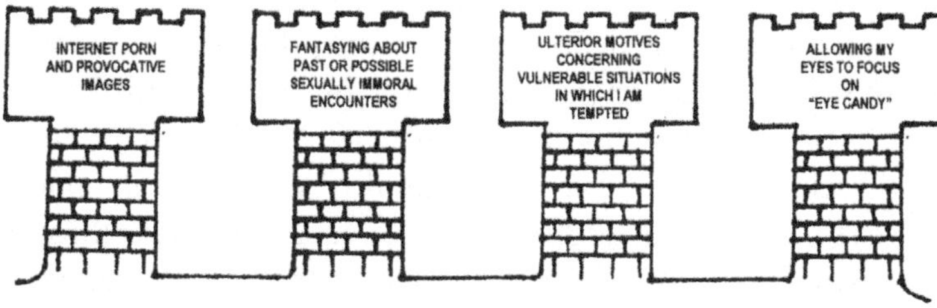

Build as many towers as you need. I have several more than what I have listed. For instance, there is a certain cologne I no longer choose to wear because I strongly associate its fragrance with the sexually immoral lifestyle I once lived. (It is amazing how a certain fragrance can serve as an *ungodly intake* for my spirit and "trigger" my mind to move in the wrong direction).

Listen, I realize we cannot entirely avoid sexually immoral influences in our day-to-day lives. I guess we could all pack up and move to Greenland, but even there we are sure to find a cozy little igloo which has access to Internet pornography. We do not need to get so hypersensitive toward our sex-saturated world that we believe the only way of overcoming sexual addiction is to become reclusive and join a monastery.

Some well-intentioned Christians might say that the recovered sexual addict should not have Internet access at all; we should not own a television or go to the movies; we should not get involved in any sort of ministry which might require us to be in a sexually tempting or vulnerable situation; we must shield ourselves from *all* possible temptation. These extremes are not necessarily called for.

Any method of recovery and restoration from sexual addiction which suggest veiling the addict from all forms of sexual temptation is a method which is sure to malfunction. In reality, this approach most always sets us up for a major relapse.

Sure, I should have filters and accountability in place when accessing the Internet. I should be very selective about what I watch on television or at the movie theater. I should not place myself in a potentially vulnerable situation when ministering (or otherwise) if it can be handled differently (e.g., being alone with a female, other than my wife or family member, without accountability measures in place.) However, the sexual addict cannot expect to journey through this world without coming face-to-face with sexually immoral influences and temptations; howbeit, if we are diligent to add "brick" and "mortar" to the *boundary walls* of defense within our spirit on a daily basis by *studying* and *obeying* the Bible; and if we are diligent to build specific *towers,* based on our individual struggles, we will be able to prevent ungodly spiritual intake from entering our soul/mind and gaining a stronghold.

I am sure that when the recovered sexual addict maintains a healthy spiritual condition, he could spend the day distributing gospel tracts on a nude beach and never be overcome with sexually compulsive thinking—if God called him to such a ministry.

[Note: Pretty much all beaches are "nude" beaches these days, considering the fashion trends of swimwear. Beaches with immodestly exposed female bodies are another one of my *towers.* I have not been called to the nude beach ministry. LOL!]

Please let me make clear that I am not saying we should tempt God by doing things or going places that could cause us to relapse into sexual sin. I am simply saying that if we keep our mind in Christlike condition by guarding against *ungodly* spiritual intake and feeding on *godly* spiritual intake, then we stop giving the enemy ground to "war against" our soul/mind, and we can face the day-to-day sex-saturated world with victory.

WHAT NOW?

With our *boundary walls* and *towers* in place, we must maintain them on a daily basis. I know there are certain things I need to especially be alert and watchful about. There are many occasions when I spot a source of temptation related to one of my "towers" and I just need to get away from that source:

> *"Can a man scoop fire into his lap and not be burned?"*
>
> (Proverbs 6:27 [NLT])

> *"Run from anything that stimulates youthful lust..."*
>
> (2 Timothy 2:22 [NLT])

Sometimes I can avoid a source of temptation by simply turning my eyes to look in another direction:

> *"I made a covenant with my eyes not to look with lust upon a young woman."*
>
> (Job 31:1 [NLT])

> *"I will set no wicked thing before mine eyes: I hate the work of them that turn aside; it shall not cleave to me."*
>
> (Psalm 101:3)

Guard your mind above all else by "feeding" your soul with God-honoring spiritual intake through studying and obeying the Bible **daily**.

This is what it takes to maintain your *boundary walls*. Also, keep alert and watchful by manning your *towers* for danger, based on your own individual struggles.

Keep in mind that the objective of these practical applications listed in this book is to detonate the ongoing revival of active and operative Holy Spirit power in our lives when it comes to defeating the besetting sin of sexual addiction. As we diligently study and obey His Word daily, the power of God is transforming our soul/spiritual mind. As we stay alert and watchful against attack (see *1 Peter 5:8*), it is God's power that protects the "city of our soul".

> *"Unless the LORD builds a house, the work of the builders is useless. Unless the Lord protects a city, guarding it with sentries will do no good."*
>
> (Psalm 127:1 [NLT])

DIABOLICAL TACTICS

The remainder of this chapter is somewhat parenthetical. However, I believe it needs to be interjected as a means of exposing one of the most diabolical tactics used by our enemy these days when it comes to the spread of sexual immorality. The terminus of Satan's scheme is the decomposition of biblical morality by way of globally pervasive and prevailing sexually immoral anarchy. His tactic? The *objectifying of females* within the mind of all mankind.

If Satan could convince one global generation that females are mere *objects* for sexual pleasure; if the adversary could persuade one global generation that females are simply *objects* to be treated as subservient beings which could be used up and discarded; if the old devil could induce one global generation to believe that females are only *objects* to exploit for sensual gratification; then Satan could gain the stronghold he needs for seducing the second generation, third generation, and so on until sexually immoral anarchy is globally pervasive and prevailing, and biblical morality is replaced with the doctrine of hedonism.

The objectifying of females is certainly nothing new. We can look back through millennia of corridors in time and observe the staggering customs and practices which divested females of any value and purpose except that of being servile sexual objects. Thus, someone might ask: *What makes our particular period of time so pivotal to Satan's scheme of replacing biblical morality with globally pervasive and prevailing sexually immoral anarchy?* I'll tell you what makes our era so crucial to Satan's stratagem: We live in the epoch of world-wide Internet access, world- wide satellite television and radio communications, instant world-wide dissemination of information.

The demonic *principalities, powers, rulers of the darkness of this world, and spiritual wickedness in high places* are now equipped like never before in history to dispense *doctrines of devils* to a global generation at one and the same time, almost as if Satan has obtained a type of "technological omnipresence":

> *"...The world around us is under the power and control of the evil one."*
>
> (1 John 5:19 [NLT])

One of the foremost doctrines of devils being globally advanced in an effort to reinforce the objectifying of females is the *theory of evolution*. Think about it: This hypothesis tries to explain that life originated billions of years ago within a "prebiotic soup" of atmospheric gases. Supposedly, the gaseous environment produced electrical flashes which united amino acids, ultimately forming the primordial stages of life. The myth goes on to insist that over extensive gamuts of time random mutations of DNA led to complete changes in the form and structure of organisms which brought forth countless diversifications of life. Essentially, the *theory of evolution* cultivates the doctrine that says: *Life as we know it originated by some fluky random forces of chance.*

The underlying counterpart to this doctrine of devils is the idea that there is no God (i.e., atheism). Thus, if there is no God, human beings were not creatively designed, and by conclusion, have no real value and purpose of existence.

The more deeply a global generation is indoctrinated with this deceit, the more we are going to witness global atrophy in the value and purpose of life. I can assure you that with a deterioration in the value and purpose of life we will behold the consequential increase in sex crimes, sex-trafficking of women and children, abortions, as well as the advancing surge of females being viewed as valueless and purposeless *abased objects* of sexual gratification to be used up and discarded.

We do not have to look far within the American culture to encounter the objectifying of females that has already forged a pervasive and prevailing stronghold in our mental inclinations. Reactionary evidence to this mentality is easily seeable in the obsessively popular drift of females striving to become *objects* of desire by augmenting their breasts and surgically reconstructing their bodies in an effort to live up to the idealistic (and very unrealistic) version of what a female must "allegedly" be in order to have real value and purpose. It is a fact that escalating numbers of preadolescent and adolescent females are suffering from self-esteem, self-concept, and self-confidence issues because they sense they are not "pretty enough" or are not "built the right way" in comparison to that unrealistic *object of desire* they feel pressured to become. We Christians need to counterpoise the world's deceptive beliefs and guiding principles with the Word of God:

> *"Charm is deceptive, and beauty does not last; but a woman who fears the Lord will be greatly praised."*
>
> (Proverbs 31:30 [NLT])

It is so very important for those of us who have recovered from sexual addiction to not buy into the world's way of objectifying females. Every time we see a female, we must remember that she is God's creation and not some fluke of godless forces which evolved into an *object* for sexual gratification. She is a masterpiece of God and has priceless value and purpose in life. She is not an *object* to be used up and replaced. In fact, she is to be treated with an uncorrupted and honorable dignity.

Our culture exhibits females as *objects* of sexual pleasure. Inferentially, our culture is an advocate of the Darwinist dogma that says: *Life as we know it originated from some fluky random forces, there is no God who intelligently and creatively designed human beings with a divine value and purpose of existence. Thus, be as hedonistic and sexually immoral as possible because tomorrow we cease to live!*

Both males and females were intelligently and creatively designed by God with a priceless value and purpose in mind:

> *"You made all the delicate, inner parts of my body and knit me together in my mother's womb. Thank you for making me so wonderfully complex! Your workmanship is marvelous—and how well I know it. You watched me as I was being formed in utter seclusion, as I was woven together in the dark of the womb. You saw me before I was born. Every day of my life was recorded in your book.*

> *Every moment was laid out before a single day had passed. How precious are Your thoughts about me, O God! They are innumerable!"*
>
> (Psalm 139:13-17 [NLT])

I realize that, due to the fall of mankind and entrance of sin into the world, our human bodies are not flawless like Adam's and Eve's when they were created. However, that does not change the fact that *all* people are the wonderfully complex, marvelous workmanship of God. It is not an evolutionary fluke that a human embryo encases the entire DNA blueprint of a marvelously intricate person for whom God has a divine plan and purpose—regardless of the circumstances into which the person is born. When an embryo or fetus is aborted, so is an astonishingly elaborate and enthralling plan and purpose of God for that preborn person's life.

The next time you are tempted to look at a female as a provocative and erotic *object* of sexually immoral gratification (this also applies to you female readers and the way you might objectify males), remember that you are looking at a person God treasures enough to die for on a cruel bloody cross. You are looking at a person God purposed and planned to exist. Even if that person is lost in sin and intentionally leads *a sexually suggestive and sexually taunting lifestyle, do not buy into that objectifying mindset*. God still loves that person and wants to see them delivered from their immorality—"pray for" them, don't "prey on" them.

THINK ON THESE

When my mind tries to gravitate toward sexually objectifying a female, I simply say a little prayer in my heart: *That is your daughter, Lord. Cleanse my thoughts and help me see her through Your eyes.* Then, in addition to that prayer, I very often "sing" (not necessarily out loud) a verse of Scripture I have put to melody:

> *"Whatsoever be true, whatsoever be honest, whatsoever be just, whatsoever be pure, whatsoever be lovely, of good report; if there be any virtue, if there be any praise,* ***think*** *on these."*
>
> (Philippians 4:8)

I sing it *repeatedly* as many times as necessary until the sanctifying truth of God's Word sets my *mind* apart to the place of holiness in which it is supposed to be. (see *John 17:17*)

Put your own melody to those divinely inspired words of God and use this method as a weapon of warfare (i.e.; "*...the sword of the Spirit, which is the word of God.*" Ephesians 6:17) as you guard your mind above all else.

PRACTICAL HOLINESS CHECKLIST

(For Personal Study and Discussion with Accountability Friends)

Practical Application # 3: Guard your mind above all else.

1. Do I "feed" on *godly spiritual intake*, or do I tend to "feed" more on ungodly spiritual intake?

   Remember, the things you allow into your *spirit* go directly to your *soul* (i.e., spiritual mind). The condition of your soul/spiritual mind influences your bodily/external choices and behavior.

   If you are deliberate enough in allowing your *spirit* to feed on godly spiritual intake, then your *soul* will continue developing in a Christlike condition and will be reflected in sexually pure physical/external choices and behavior with your *body*. (see *Proverbs 4:23; Ephesians 4:22,23; Romans 13:12-14; Galatians 5:16*)

2. Am I establishing a *boundary wall* within my spirit that defines and limits the kind of spiritual intake allowed to enter?

   Remember, our *boundary walls* must be constructed with the "brick" and "mortar" of the inspired and infallible Word of God. The *Bible* is the "brick" we are to use in constructing the walls while *obedience* to the Bible is the "mortar" which holds our walls together. (see *Luke 6:47,48; James 1:22*)

   The Word of God is alive and powerful enough to penetrate and engrave itself into the innermost merging point of the spirit and soul. That is where your *boundary walls* will be constructed. (see *Hebrews 4:12*)

   If your spiritual diet does not include a daily intake of God's Word, and obedience to His Word, you are not constructing a solid boundary wall and your soul will become like an undefended city which is open to any method of attack: (see *Proverbs 25:28*; *James 1:14,15*)

Sexual temptation presents the bait; the addict takes the bait as compulsive preoccupation is incited within the mind; the addict then manifests sexually immoral action through his bodily/external choices and behavior.

As a result, death (i.e., ruptured and broken communion with the Spirit of God) is produced in the sexual addict's life.

3. Am I building *towers* atop my boundary walls?

   Remember, these *towers* serve as guardhouses which keep you alert to the potential dangers of temptation which threaten your sexual purity.

   Based on your own individual struggles with sexual immorality, what are the strategic "towers" you need to have in place atop your boundary walls?

   Remember, there are certain things you need to especially be alert and watchful about. There are going to be many occasions when you spot a source of temptation related to one of your "towers" and you just need to get away from that source or avert your eyes. (see *Proverbs 6:27; 2 Timothy 2:22; Job 31:1; Psalm 101:3*)

4. Am I maintaining my *boundary walls* and *towers* on a daily basis?

   Remember, guard your mind above all else by "feeding" your soul with God-honoring spiritual intake through studying and obeying the Bible **daily**. This is what it takes to maintain your "boundary walls". Also, keep alert and watchful by manning your "towers" **daily** for danger, based on your own individual struggles.

As you diligently study and obey His word *daily*, the power of God is transforming your soul/spiritual mind. As you stay alert and watchful against attack, it is God's power that protects the "city" of your soul. (see *Psalm 127:1*)

5. Do I tend to buy into the world's view of objectifying females?

Remember, every female is a creation of God and not some fluke of godless forces which evolved into an "object" for your sexual gratification. She is a masterpiece of God and has priceless value and purpose in life. She is to be treated with an uncorrupted and honorable dignity.

The next time you are tempted to look at a female as a provocative and erotic "object" of sexually immoral gratification (this also applies to you female readers and the way you might objectify males), remember that you are looking at a person God treasures enough to die for on a cruel, bloody cross.

When your mind tries to gravitate toward sexually objectifying a female: Say this prayer: 'Lord, that is your daughter. Cleanse my thoughts and help me see her through Your eyes.'

Repeatedly rehearse or "sing" verses of Scripture from your heart until the sanctifying truth of God's Word sets your mind apart to the place of holiness in which it is supposed to be. (e.g. *Philippians 4:8*)

~ Chapter Nine ~

Daily Deployment

Practical Application # 4: Deploy a daily spiritual program for battle.

We often hear the word "deploy" used in reference to military operations. The idea, of course, being that of dispatching troops in an effort to form a line of defense and/or offense for battle.

As we study the fourth and final application of practical holiness in this book, I would like for you to understand that the word "deploy" has similar military connotation as we use it in connection with a *daily spiritual program for battle.* It is no secret that we Christians are in active combat with a demonic spiritual realm which devotes sustained effort toward manipulating and provoking the impulses of our sinful nature in union with worldly influences:

> *"For we are not fighting against people made of flesh and blood, but against the evil rulers and authorities of the unseen world, against those mighty powers of darkness who rule this world, and against wicked spirits in the heavenly realms."*
>
> (Ephesians 6:12 [NLT])

Therefore, our defensive and offensive program for battle against these hostile and threatening forces must be waged within the spiritual realm as well.

I must *deploy* a combined "battalion" of spiritual forces on a daily basis to form my line of defense/offense for engagement with the enemy.

The combined battalion of spiritual forces I must deploy as a daily spiritual program for battle is fourfold:

I. Quality time of prayer communion with God
II. Quality time of Bible study
III. Quality time of fellowship with other Christians
IV. Quality time of exercising spiritual gifts

A daily spiritual program for battle which persistently assimilates all four of these practices will generate a spiritual force against which the demonic realm does not have a fighting chance. The active and operative power of God's Holy Spirit is detonated in an explosive manner within the Christian's life by unyieldingly exercising these daily disciplines.

Notice the words "*quality time*" at the beginning of each discipline. "Quality time" does not necessarily mean that we must spend hours of time practicing these activities; there is a difference between *quality* time and *quantity* time.

While "quantity" time places greatest importance on volume or portion of time, "quality" time focuses on the *exclusiveness* of time we devote to nurturing these four disciplines. Now don't get me wrong. If you are able to devote hours upon hours of your day to these spiritual activities, that is great! Howbeit, most people are not situated in such a fashion that they can spend an hour or two in prayer, then an hour or two in Bible study, then an hour or two in fellowshipping, then an hour or two exercising their spiritual gifts—at least not on a daily basis. Hence, we need to center our daily commitment to these practices on their *quality* instead of the measure or portion of time we commit.

You see, it is so easy to get caught up in the mindset that thinks, I just can't find time for devoting myself to prayer each day! I can't find time for Bible study, fellowshipping, and exercising my spiritual gifts every day! So, what do we tend to do? We tend to think, Maybe I'll find some time tomorrow. Then we do nothing: no prayer, no Bible study, no fellowshipping, no exercising our spiritual gifts. We save those things for Sunday mornings and

Wednesday evenings; and even then we, too often, perform those activities as a monotonous series of languid routine.

I have discovered that *finding* quality time to nurture these spiritual disciplines is truly next to impossible on a daily basis; thus, I must *make* quality time in order to successfully deploy a **daily** spiritual program for battle. If that means I can only spend an hour or less with each of these disciplines on most days, then I need to make sure that the hour or less I spend is quality time—devoted *exclusively* to nurturing and cultivating my relationship with God in prayer; devoted *exclusively* to nurturing and cultivating my relation with God in Bible study; devoted *exclusively* to nurturing and cultivating deeper relationships with other Christians through fellowship; devoted *exclusively* to nurturing and cultivating my spiritual gifts for the benefit of the church by exercising those gifts. Regardless of the amount of time spent in each of these areas, *exclusive devotion* equals *quality time* when it comes to practicing these four spiritual disciplines.

I. QUALITY TIME OF PRAYER COMMUNION WITH GOD

Prayer is possibly the most neglected resource we have been blessed with as children of God. In fact, communion with God through prayer is a miraculous privilege that is not accessible to the non-Christian. It is not that God does not want to hear the prayers of a non-Christian; rather, it is just a spiritual fact that sin separates the unsaved person from communion with God. The good news is that by grace through faith in Jesus Christ, a person can become a Christian—a child of God—and be transplanted from a *position of enmity* with God to a *position of peace* with God. Hallelujah!

> *"Therefore, since we have been made right in God's sight by faith, we have* ***peace with God*** *because of what Jesus Christ our Lord has done for us. Because of our faith, Christ has*

> *brought us into* ***this place of highest privilege*** *where we now stand, and we confidently and joyfully look forward to sharing God's glory."*
>
> (Romans 5:1,2 [NLT])

By grace through faith in Jesus Christ, a "peace treaty" has been put into effect between the Christian and God, justified on the authority of Christ's shed blood for our sins:

> *"In whom we have redemption through his blood, the forgiveness of sins, according to the riches of his grace."*
>
> (Ephesians 1:7)

The price that was paid for our privilege to commune with God in prayer is the shed blood of our Savior Jesus Christ. That in itself makes the entitlement of prayer beyond the value of any other price which could possibly exist. What a possession of inestimable worth we have in connecting with God through prayer. The connection fee has been paid for by the very blood of God!

Perhaps when we get to our heavenly home, we will have a complete understanding of prayer. At that point I think most of us will realize we should have given prayer the greater place of primacy in our Christian journey while we were on earth.

Jesus is the One who set the standard for us when it comes to prayer:

> *"And in the morning, rising up a great while before day, he went out, and departed into a solitary place, and there prayed."*
>
> (Mark 1:35)

He shows us the importance of exclusive devotion when it comes to quality time of prayer communion with God. What are some of the things this verse teaches us about exclusive devotion to prayer communion with God?

A. ***Exclusive devotion*** to prayer communion with His Father began Jesus' day with seeking His instruction and guidance. The Bible is replete with special importance placed on early morning prayer communion:

> *"O God, thou art my God;* ***early will I seek thee****: my soul thirsteth for thee, my flesh longeth for thee in a dry and thirsty land, where no water is; To see thy power and thy glory, so as I have seen thee in the sanctuary."*
>
> (Psalm 63:1,2)

> *"...****Morning by morning*** *he wakens me and opens my understanding to his will. The Sovereign* LORD *has spoken to me, and I have listened. I do not rebel or turn away."*
>
> (Isaiah 50:4,5 [NLT])

God fills our cup with His wisdom, instruction, guidance, and power to navigate the day ahead of us if we will commune with Him as *first priority*.

B. ***Exclusive devotion*** to prayer communion with God is not a question of personal convenience but rather self-discipline and commitment to a relationship. Notice Christ's example of this kind of self-disciplined sacrifice in Mark 1:35—

> *"...rising up a great while before day..."*

It may have been more convenient for Jesus to press the proverbial "snooze button", but he chose to rise up and *make* time for exclusive devotion in prayer communion with His Father.

C. ***Exclusive devotion*** to prayer communion with God should be free from distraction or diverted concentration:

> *"...[Jesus] went out, and departed into a solitary place, and there prayed."*
>
> (Mark 1:35)

What I am about to tell you might sound strange, but I actually insert earplugs into my ears during my daily prayer time. It really helps me keep my mind fixed on communion with the Lord when all I can hear is the prayerful conversation I am having with God.

Let me give you an example: If you are able to, take your hands and use each forefinger to plug your ears. Are they plugged? Okay, now in a soft voice say, "Good morning Lord." Did you hear that? (You can unplug your ears now.) All you could hear was the voice of your prayer inside your head—no other distractions to divert your concentration.

My "earplug method" is obviously not necessary for having an effective prayer focus (I doubt Jesus used earplugs), but it does help me maintain a sharply defined concentration as I pray. If you think this might be helpful for you too, a pair of comfortable earplugs are really inexpensive.

However we choose to free ourselves from distraction and diverted concentration as we give exclusive devotion to prayer communion with God, the important thing is that we deploy this quality time of prayer as part of our spiritual program for battle on a *daily basis*. Jesus warns:

> ***"Keep alert and pray****. Otherwise, temptation will overpower you. For though the spirit is willing enough, the body is weak!"*
>
> (Matthew 26:41 [NLT])

The active and operative power of God's Holy Spirit flows through a *daily* prayer life. In fact, I have learned to keep a pad of paper and pencil nearby as I pray because, as we *develop* our daily prayer lives, God will communicate things to us by His "still small voice". One of the things I jotted down during a prayer session as I heard from God:

"If you will be persistent in your daily prayer commitment, I [God] will processionally reveal to you the true power of prayer."

I received that illumination of truth and began practicing a *persistent daily prayer commitment*. Just as God promised, He began revealing to me the true power of prayer.

> *"...the earnest prayer of a righteous person has* ***great power*** *and* ***wonderful results****."*
>
> (James 5:16 [NLT])

II. QUALITY TIME OF BIBLE STUDY

Exclusive devotion to daily Bible study has a tremendous transforming influence on our soul/spiritual mind. The Word of God is the best "food" our spirit can digest and absorb for the nourishment of our soul. The inspired Word of God is referred to as *"...sweeter than honey, even honey dripping from the comb."* (Psalm 19:10 [NLT])

Jeremiah speaks of God's inspired Word as sustaining food:

> *"Thy words were found, and* ***I did eat them****; and thy word was unto me the joy and rejoicing of mine heart: for I am called by thy name, O LORD God of hosts."*
>
> (Jeremiah 15:16)

Ezekiel was commanded to eat a scroll (i.e., the Word of God) as part of a vision he experienced:

> *"...'Son of man, eat what I am giving you—* ***eat this scroll****! Then go and give its message to the people of Israel...* ***Eat it all****,' he said. And when I ate it, it tasted as sweet as honey."*
>
> (Ezekiel 3:1,3 [NLT])

Obviously we are not to *literally* eat our Bible; however, we are to "feed" on it in the sense of *internalizing* its layers of truth so we become less controlled by the power of our sinful nature, and progressively transformed by the renewing of our mind:

> *"Then he added, 'Son of man, let all my words sink deep into your own heart first. Listen to them carefully for yourself.'"*
>
> (Ezekiel 3:10 [NLT])

Before I can *externally* live victoriously over sexual addiction in my day-to-day life, I must *internally* "feed" on the Bible in my day-to-day life:

> *"Thy word have I hid in mine heart, that I might not sin against thee."*
>
> (Psalm 119:11)

I can assure you that the more persistently you develop the **daily** habit of feeding on God's Word, the more your spiritual appetite will increase. However, you can never exhaust the fulfilling richness of Scripture that satisfies your hunger.

One of my favorite verses in the Bible, pertaining to "feeding" on God's Word, is *Psalm 1:2*—

> *"But his [the Christian's] delight is in the law [instructions] of the LORD; and in his law [instructions] doth he meditate day and night."*
>
> (brackets mine)

Notice the word *"meditate"* in that verse. The original Hebrew of that word brings with it the thought of *chewing* on the Word of God; gleaning all of the flavor and nutrients from it that we can.

Also notice the words *"day and night"*. In other words, there should not be a 24-hour span of time that we allow to pass by without spending some *exclusive devotion* "feeding" on God's nutritious Word, providing the spiritual sustenance necessary for spiritual health and Holy Spirit empowerment over sexual addiction.

> *"And he shall be like a tree planted by the rivers of water, that bringeth forth his fruit in*

his season; his leaf also shall not wither; and whatsoever he doeth shall prosper."

(Psalm 1:3)

The Bible also teaches us that if we "*walk*" in the Holy Spirit of God, we will be empowered to overcome the drive of our sinful nature:

"This I say then, Walk in the Spirit, and ye shall not fulfill the lust of the flesh."

(Galatians 5:16)

I just want to say that "walking in the Spirit" has *everything* to do with "feeding" on the Word of God.

The word "walk" is figurative of our entire lifestyle as Christians, and the fact that we should be making forward progress, step-by-step in our spiritual journey toward Christlikeness. When the Word of God says I am to take this "walk" *in the Spirit*, it simply means that the capability and effectiveness I need in order to successfully continue moving forward each day comes from my willing reliance upon the Holy Spirit of God. Well, what is the central route by which the Holy Spirit delivers strength and power for our daily spiritual "walk"? That's right, it is by way of His Holy Spirit inspired Word—the Bible.

"All Scripture is inspired by God and is useful to teach us what is true and to make us realize what is wrong in our lives. It straightens us out and teaches us to do what is right. It is God's way of preparing us in every way, fully equipped for every good thing God wants us to do."

(2 Timothy 3:16,17 [NLT])

The Bible is not just some motivational self-help book designed by men for mental and emotional stimulation. My friend, the Bible is the *only* book that is miraculously God-breathed for everlasting preservation as the inerrant, infallible Word of God that He Himself delivered to mankind through mankind.

The Bible is not a dead and obsolete literary composition. If you have a Bible nearby, please pick it up. Go ahead, just pick it up and hold it in your hand. I am holding my Bible in my left hand as I write this page. As you hold your Bible, and I hold mine, just take a look at what we have in our hands. The canon of Scripture in the Bible (i.e. 39 Old Testament books, 27 New Testament books) will be preserved for all of eternity ahead. Every other book in existence will eventually cease to exist, but the Scriptures, from Genesis to Revelation, will *never cease* to exist. All other books, including this one I have written on escaping sexual addiction, will one day burn into ashes (see *2 Peter 3:10*), but the spiritual contents of the Bible you and I hold in our hands will live for eternity. Do you realize the pricelessness of what we hold in our hands?

> *"...the word of God, which liveth and abideth for ever...the word of the Lord endureth for ever. And this is the word which by the gospel is preached unto you."*
>
> (1 Peter 1:23,25)

The Word of God "*liveth*". That's right, it is alive!

> *"For the word of God is full of living power..."*
>
> (Hebrews 4:12 [NLT])

Let us revive our appreciation and wonderment of the Holy Bible and the *living power* that the Holy Spirit desires to impart into our soul for victory over the demonic realm, our sinful nature, and the influences of worldliness.

The Word of God is able to sanctify and set us apart from worldliness. Jesus revealed this as He prayed to the Father for you and me:

> *"Sanctify them through thy truth: thy word is truth."*

(John 17:17)

That is fantastic news for the Christian who struggles with sexual addiction. The more we persistently draw near to God through *exclusive devotion* in daily Bible study, the more empowered and set-apart to Him we are for holy, victorious living. Praise God!

Developing the habit of deploying quality time in Bible study as part of your spiritual program for battle on a daily basis really only requires a Bible and prayer. Nevertheless, I recommend that you get a commentary of the Old and New Testaments that will help you to have a practical understanding of Scripture. A pastor, minister, or chaplain can usually suggest good Bible study reference books which will help you dig into the depths of God's Word on a daily basis.

Memorization of Scripture is also vital to Bible study and getting the living power of God's Word into your heart. When I am in the process of memorizing a verse, I write it on a tiny piece of paper or index card and carry it with me in my shirt pocket where I can take time to review it throughout the day. For example:

(Psalm 119:11)
THY WORD HAVE I HID IN MINE HEART,
THAT I MIGHT NOT SIN AGAINST THEE.
(Psalm 119:11)

As you can see, I placed the "address" (i.e., Psalm 119:11) at the beginning and the ending of the verse. By memorizing the "address" of the verse at the beginning and ending (as if it is part of the verse) you will have a better chance of recalling verses and where they are located as you increase the amount of verses memorized.

Once I have a verse memorized, I add the "address" to the list of other verses I already have memorized. For instance:

John 20:31

2 Corinthians 7:10
Galatians 2:20
Psalm 118:24
Psalm 107:2
Psalm 119:11

I keep the list of "addresses" on a piece of notebook paper inside my Bible so I can "rehearse" verses each day before or after my Bible study time. Oftentimes I even take my list of "addresses" and practice them as I do my physical exercise routine. (There is just something about meditating on memorized Scripture while exercising the body that brings greater spiritual clarity.)

Once you have memorized a great deal of Scripture you will have several columns of "addresses" listed on the notebook paper. When you have so many verses memorized, you will not have the time to rehearse them all at one sitting before your Bible study time. At least incorporate the rehearsal of some of them, then pick up the next day where you left off. You will be amazed by the impact and empowerment that the memorized Word of God has in your life.

[Note: As Carol Jean Blakely—the editor of this book—was working on this portion of the manuscript, she made a very helpful suggestion concerning the verses you are memorizing: When you have time, begin to divide your memorized verses (by address) into categories that will help you when you have a specific need. For example, when you are feeling lonely and depressed; when you need comforting or need to comfort someone (perhaps after some bad news); when you need extra strength because the devil is poking at your weak spots and reminding you of your past; when you have a task that seems impossible; when God is prompting you to do or say something.]

III. QUALITY TIME OF FELLOWSHIP WITH OTHER CHRISTIANS

Exclusive devotion to fellowship with other Christians on a daily basis may simply involve a phone call in which you discuss what is on your heart, and pray for each other. Or, perhaps it includes meeting with two or more fellow Christians each day for a devotional time of Scripture and prayer. Regardless of how you choose to exercise quality time of fellowship with other Christians on a daily basis, the important thing is that you are firm in its deployment as part of your daily spiritual program for battle:

> *"But exhort one another* ***daily****, while it is called Today; lest any of you be hardened through the deceitfulness of sin."*
>
> (Hebrews 3:13)

To "*exhort*" one another means to *persuade*, *urge*, even *warn* each other as Christians through **daily** fellowship, in an effort to help each other continue in following a specific course of action. The specific course of action in which we are to "exhort" one another to continue is: *our belief in the Lord Jesus Christ and all the instructions that the Bible teaches us to apply in our lives as a result of our belief.*

Notice what this verse teaches us about the constancy of our fellowship: "*But exhort one another daily...*" When the infallible, verbally inspired Bible (which is the all-sufficient rule of faith and practice in our lives) places emphasis on doing something "**daily**", we should not shrug it off as a trivial command. There is indispensible Holy Spirit power that flows into our soul as a result of daily fellowship with other Christians.

Why do I need this Holy Spirit power through daily fellowship with other Christians?

> *"...lest any of you be hardened through the deceitfulness of sin."*
>
> (Hebrews 3:13)

The "natural default mode" of human beings is to be "*hardened through the deceitfulness of sin.*" That is one of the main reasons it is so easy for a sexual addict to retrogress into his former sexually immoral bearing when he discontinues the deployment of a daily spiritual program for battle. In fact, such retrograde almost always steers the addict into deepeningly worse sexually immoral thinking and conduct than previously practiced.

We see that *Hebrews 3:13* actually personified "sin" by saying it is "deceitful". When a person deceives you, they are giving you a *false impression* about something. That is exactly what sin has done to so many of us sexual addicts; it has given us *false impressions* to rationalize certain sexually immoral choices we have made, and certain paths we have taken as being the most fulfilling. Those false impressions are a lie!

The "*deceitfulness of sin*" sells us the false impression of itself through a hedonistic philosophy (i.e., the doctrine that teaches personal pleasure and self-gratification as the highest good in life). A sobriquet of this philosophy could be called: *The Greener Grass Doctrine*—that is, "*The grass is always greener on the other side!*" There is an evangelist friend of mine named Galen Yoder who once said, "The only reason the grass is greener on the other side of the fence is because the grass is planted on top of a septic tank!"

I could personally identify with what he was saying because, when I was a kid, our backyard had a septic tank buried in it. Sure enough the grass growing in that part of the yard was always greener than the rest of the lawn because of the seepage from the tank below.

Dad told me not to play in that part of the yard; however, the grass was just too inviting for a barefoot boy. I well remember the day I ventured into the alluring greener grass. At first the delicate blades of verdure felt soft and refreshing as they passed like silken feathers of pleasure between my toes and the soles of my feet. *Dad must not know what he's talking about! This grass is great!* , I thought to myself. My risky undertaking was paying off as I confidently proceeded further in.

Then it happened! Something went terribly wrong! My feet began sinking in the sewage-saturated soil as if I had become ensnared by some fiendish hands from below. As I yanked my feet upward and made a run for it, the swampy ooze yielded additionally under my weight until I was ankle-deep and had fallen into the rancid bog. I had to crawl the remainder of my way out of that area of the yard until I was again on solid ground. Mom made me shed my clothes and take a thorough rinsing with the waterhose before I could go into the house.

The spiritual application of that experience is so strong when we think of the "*deceitfulness of sin*" and how it gives us the false impression of itself by making the sinful pleasures of this world appear so much "greener" than serving Jesus Christ. So often I have ventured into these "greener grasses" of ungodly pleasure and found myself bogged down in the "sewage of sin" because I believed the false impression it gives of itself.

Hebrews 3:13 also teaches us that there is a "hardening" effect which takes place in our lives as an outcome of the "deceitfulness of sin":

> *"...lest any of you be* ***hardened*** *through the deceitfulness of sin."*

In the original Greek, the word translated "hardened" paints us a picture of the nape of one's neck stiffening, rendering the head in an unbending position. The spiritual implication is that the "deceitfulness of sin" takes us to a place where our heart becomes *unbending* to the Lordship of Jesus Christ. Instead, "sin" becomes the governing power in our lives—even as Christians.

Now do you have a better understanding of *Hebrews 3:13* and the reason we need God's Holy Spirit power flowing into our lives through daily fellowship with other Christians? For the sexual addict, the power of God's Holy Spirit, which becomes active and operative in our lives through daily fellowship with other Christians, protects us from the deception and truth-blinding nature of sin which desires to govern our lives and shift us back to our natural default mode of self-defeating and self-destructive sexually immoral conduct.

As I close on this particular spiritual discipline, let me add that I have often had people ask me whether we really have to fellowship within church assemblies in order to be "obedient" Christians. Well, allow me to simply say that the Bible clearly teaches all Christians are members of the Church in its *universal* sense. Every person who receives Jesus Christ as Lord and Savior between the time of Pentecost in *Acts 2* and the Rapture mentioned in *1 Thessalonians 4:16,17* is a member of the Church in its "universal" sense. This "universal" Church is what the Bible refers to as "The Body of Christ". The apostle Paul writes:

> *"Christ is the head of the church, which is his body...I am glad when I suffer for you in my body, for I am completing what remains of Christ's sufferings for his body, the church."*
>
> (Colossians 1:18, 24[NLT])

While it would be totally impossible for every person of the "universal" body of Christians to assemble together at one location at the very same time (at least not until after the Rapture), the Bible does teach (and even commands) us to assemble ourselves together in *local* church gatherings.

Some of the primary reasons an "obedient" Christian will assemble himself together in fellowship with a *local* church include:

A. Hearing the Word of God

The early Christians met in local church assemblies where they:

> *"...continued steadfastly in* ***the apostles' doctrine..."***
>
> (Acts 2:42)

Their local church fellowship included coming together to hear "the apostles' doctrine" (i.e., the inspired Word of God) preached.

Get involved with a local church assembly that has a pastor who teaches and preaches the Bible. If you are hearing *less* Bible, and *more* of a "secular motivational oratory" being delivered from the pulpit, go find a local church that preaches the Bible. Otherwise, your ears may be soothed, but your faith will wither. (see *2 Timothy 4:2,3*)

B. Fellowship

The indispensible importance of fellowship with other Christians has already been discussed in this chapter. The Bible clearly teaches us that fellowship is part of what we should do as members of a local church assembly:

> *"And they continued steadfastly in the apostles' doctrine and* ***fellowship****..."*
>
> (Acts 2:42)

There is a massive detonation of God's active and operative Holy Spirit power in our lives when we come together in community with other Christians in our local church. Besides, we are commanded to do so:

> *"Not forsaking the assembling of ourselves together, as the manner of some is; but exhorting one another: and so much the more, as ye see the day approaching."*
>
> (Hebrews 10:25)

C. The Breaking of Bread

In a local church assembly, we are to break bread together:

> *"And they continued steadfastly in the apostles' doctrine and fellowship, and in* ***breaking of bread****..."*
>
> (Acts 2:42)

Sharing common meals together with other Christians is an incredibly bonding experience; nevertheless, the Lord's Supper is being referred to here. We know that the early Christians observed the Lord's Supper (i.e., communion) when they came together as members of their local church assemblies on Sundays. (see *Acts 20:7*)

D. Prayers

The local church assembly should be a fellowship of Christians who make praying together a priority:

> *"And they continued steadfastly in the apostles' doctrine and fellowship, and in breaking of bread, and **in prayers**."*
>
> (Acts 2:42)

The power of local Bible-believing Christian church assemblies who pray together with fervency witness the miraculous response to their complete dependence on God. Jesus said:

> *"...My house shall be called the **house of prayer**..."*
>
> (Matthew 21:13)

Every local church should be called a "house of prayer".

We could go on and discuss the local church assembly's role in evangelism, baptism, the realm of corporate worship, etc.; nonetheless, I hope I at least touched on enough about the importance of membership within a *local* church assembly to clarify the fact that in order to be an "obedient" Christian, the answer is, "Yes, we must become active members of a local church fellowship."

IV. QUALITY TIME EXERCISING SPIRITUAL GIFTS

If you are a Christian, you have a spiritual gift. Even the person who became a Christian a few seconds ago has a spiritual gift, regardless of how young or old that new Christian may be:

> *"A spiritual gift is given to each of us as a means of helping the entire church."*
>
> (1 Corinthians 12:7 [NLT])

> *"...[God] has given each one of us a special gift according to the generosity of Christ."*
>
> (Ephesians 4:7 [NLT] brackets mine)

> *"God has given gifts to each of you from his great variety of spiritual gifts. Manage them well so that God's generosity can flow through you."*
>
> (1 Peter 4:10 [NLT])

You may possibly receive other spiritual gifts later in your Christian journey, but one thing is sure: you received *at least one* spiritual gift at the moment you received Jesus Christ as your Lord and Savior.

Perhaps you already possessed inherent skills or talents prior to becoming a Christian. If so, God often transfigures those aptitudes into spiritual gifts when you receive Jesus Christ as Lord and Savior.

It is also important to understand that God gives us these gifts for serving and nurturing *other* people:

> *"Don't think only of your own good. Think of other Christians and what is best for them."*
>
> (1 Corinthians 10:24 [NLT])

> *"A spiritual gift is given to each of us as a means of helping the entire church."*
>
> (1 Corinthians 12:7 [NLT])

It is the eventual ruin and setback of many Christians who have used their God-given gifts as a primary means for their own personal enrichment. Our foremost aim must be to put our gifts into action and service for the nurturing of others first. As we do this, the active and operative power of God's Holy Spirit is exquisite in degree and effect when it comes to maintaining victory over sin:

> *"The generous prosper and are satisfied; those who refresh others will themselves be refreshed."*
>
> (Proverbs 11:25 [NLT])

I am truly persuaded to believe that in many locales, the Church of God has become astronomically derelict when it comes to giving proper care and attention to the essential importance of spiritual gifts and their development in the lives of *every* Christian.

Priority needs to be given to the discovery and development of spiritual gifts within the lives of all Christians. Too many Christians are unable to tell you what their spiritual gifts are. Go ahead and ask your fellow Christians about their spiritual gifts; too many of us will say, "I'm really not sure."

Some Christians will tell you they don't know if they even have a spiritual gift. Can you imagine the fantastic and explosive impact just one local church could have on their surrounding sphere of influence within the community if *every* Christian in that church knew what their spiritual gifts are and exercised those gifts to the fullest power of God's Holy Spirit?! Hallelujah! Can you imagine the effect if *every* local church in every place made the development of spiritual gifts a priority?!

We are to be "*doers*" of the Word of God, not "*hearers only*". (see *James 1:22*) The Bible clearly instructs us what to do when it comes to spiritual gifts: We are to "*stir up*" the spiritual gift God has given us. We are not to neglect spiritual gifts and allow them to die down like the fading embers of a campfire in the engulfing darkness of a forest. Rather, we are to stir and fan our spiritual gifts until they erupt into brilliant and beaming flames hurling the light of God's love through Jesus Christ into the lives of others:

> *"This is why I remind you to fan into flames the spiritual gift God gave you..."*
>
> (2 Timothy 1:6 [NLT])

As individual Christians, when we discover, develop, and give *exclusive devotion* to exercising our spiritual gifts on a persistent basis, we are not only allowing the active and operative power of God's Holy Spirit to flow through us and into the lives of others; we are also being empowered to resist the compulsion of sin. For the recovered sexual addict, this empowerment is a necessary daily reprieve.

I realize that the word "reprieve" usually refers to a *temporary* deliverance; but the fact is, if I fail to give persistent exclusive devotion to fanning the flames of my spiritual gifts, I am putting myself at risk of being overcome by the darkness of sexual immorality.

A. How do I discover my spiritual gifts?

The New Testament records four lists of spiritual gifts: *Romans 12:6-8; 1 Corinthians 12:8-10; 28-30, Ephesians 4:11; 1 Peter 4:10,11.* It is of utmost significance for us to have a correct definition of each spiritual gift found in the Bible if we are to discover our own spiritual gifts. It is also important to understand that the spiritual gifts listed in the Bible are not an exhaustive catalogue of gifts. Additionally, it is imperative to learn which of the gifts itemized in Scripture are *sign gifts* so you can exclude them from gifts which are available to believers today. A thorough systematic treatment of spiritual gifts, their accurate definitions, and which gifts are given to Christians today can be found in a fantastic book written by Steven W. Waterhouse, ***Not by Bread Alone: An Outlined Guide to Bible Doctrine*** (3rd edition; Amarillo; Westcliff Press, 2007). The Web address for Dr. Waterhouse is www.webtheology.com. I am very grateful for Dr.

Waterhouse and what I have learned from studying his writings on systematic theology. I recommend his book as a volume which any serious Bible student will refer to again and again in their studies.

If you are a Christian who has not yet discovered your spiritual gifts, you can begin moving toward that discovery by simply becoming compliant with the common commands which are given to all Christians. For instance, you can embark on this course of discovering your spiritual gifts by looking for opportunities to offer yourself in some kind of servanthood within the local church. There is always some way for you to serve. In offering ourselves like this, we are being obedient to a standard command issued to all Christians:

> *"...that ye present your bodies a living sacrifice..."*
>
> (Romans12:1)

The more we present our lives to God through all-around servanthood, the more conscious we become about explicit affinities which lead us to the discovery of our spiritual gifts. Dr. Steven Waterhouse says it with superb clarity:

"Knowledge of specific interests arises out of a living context of servanthood. Specific direction in the Lord's work arises from general involvement in that work."
(*Not by Bread Alone: An Outlined Guide to Bible Doctrine* [3rd edition; Amarillo; Westcliff Press, 2007], p. 292)

PRACTICAL HOLINESS CHECKLIST
(For Personal Study and Discussion with Accountability Friends)

Practical Application # 4: Deploy a daily spiritual program for battle.

1. Do I honestly realize that, as a Christian, I am in active combat with a demonic spiritual realm which devotes sustained effort toward manipulating and provoking the impulses of my sinful nature in union with worldly influences?

    Your defensive and offensive program for battle against these hostile and threatening forces must be waged within the spiritual realm as well. (see *Ephesians 6:10-18*)

2. Am I deploying the fourfold battalion of spiritual forces on a daily basis: Quality time of prayer communion with God; Quality time of Bible study; Quality time of fellowship with other Christians; and, Quality time of exercising spiritual gifts?

    A daily spiritual program for battle which persistently assimilates all four of these practices will generate a spiritual power against which the demonic realm does not have a fighting chance.

    These daily practices are often referred to as spiritual disciplines because they do not come naturally and must be persistently nurtured and developed.

3. Do I give prayer communion with God the priority it should have in my life on a *daily* basis?

    Jesus began His day with exclusive devotion to prayer communion with His Father, seeking instruction and guidance.

Exclusive devotion to prayer communion with God is not a question of personal convenience but, rather, self-discipline and commitment to a relationship with your Lord and Savior, Jesus Christ.

Exclusive devotion to prayer communion with God should be free from distraction or diverted concentration. (see *Mark 1:35; Psalm 63:1,2; Matthew 26:41*)

4. Do I realize that before I can *externally* live victoriously over sexual addiction in my day-to-day life, I must first *internally* "feed" on the Bible in my day-to-day life?

   You are to "feed" on the Bible in the sense of internalizing its layers of truth so you become less controlled by the power of your sinful nature, and you become progressively transformed by the renewing of your mind.

   The central route by which the Holy Spirit delivers strength and power for your daily spiritual "walk" is by way of God's Spirit-inspired Word—the Bible.

   (see *Ezekiel 3:10; Psalm 119:133; 2 Timothy 3:16,17; Galatians 5:16*)

5. Do I have a systematic method of memorizing Scripture and rehearsing my memory verses on a daily basis?

   The memorization of Scripture is vital to Bible study and getting the living power of God's Word into your heart. (see *Psalm 119:11*)

6. Am I firm in my deployment of fellowship with other Christians as part of my daily spiritual program for battle?

   Fellowship with other Christians encourages your belief in the Lord Jesus Christ and all of the instructions that the Bible teaches you to apply in your life as a result of your belief.

There is indispensable Holy Spirit power that flows into your soul as a result of daily fellowship with other Christians. Otherwise, it is easy for you to retrogress into your former sexually immoral bearing. Such retrograde almost always steers you into deepeningly worse sexually immoral thinking and conduct than before. The power of God's Holy Spirit, which becomes active and operative through daily fellowship with other Christians, protects you from the deception and truth-blinding nature of sin which desires to govern your life and shift you back to your "natural default mode" of self-defeating and self-destructive sexually immoral conduct. (see *Hebrews 3:13*)

7. Am I obedient to the Lord's command for me to assemble myself together with other believers in *local* church gatherings on a regular basis?

   Assembling yourself together with other believers as a member of a local church strengthens you spiritually through hearing the Bible preached, sharing the intimacy of the Lord's Supper as a church family, praying together and witnessing the miraculous response to your complete dependence upon God through those prayers. You will grow stronger spiritually as you become active with your church family in worshipping God together and taking Christ's love to the local community surrounding your local church. To be an obedient Christian, you must become an active member of a local church fellowship. (see *Hebrews 10:25; Acts 2:42*)

8. Am I persistent in deploying my *spiritual gifts* as part of a daily spiritual program for battle?

When our foremost aim is to put our spiritual gifts into action and service for nurturing other people, we receive a Holy Spirit empowerment which is exquisite in degree when it comes to walking in victory over sin.

We are to never neglect our spiritual gifts. Instead, we are to stir and fan them until they erupt into brilliant and beaming spiritual flames hurling the light of God's love through Jesus Christ into the lives of others.

If you are a Christian who has not yet discovered your spiritual gifts, you can begin moving toward that discovery by simply becoming compliant with the common commands which are given to all Christians. The most ordinary way to embark on this course of discovery is by looking for opportunities to offer yourself in servanthood within the local church. The more you present your life to God through all-around servanthood, the more conscious you will become about explicit affinities which lead you to the discovery of your spiritual gifts. (see *1 Peter 4:10; 1 Corinthians 10:24; Proverbs 11:25; 1 Timothy 4:14; 2 Timothy 1:6; Romans 12:1,2*)

~ Chapter Ten ~
The Trap is Baited

In July of 2006, ten months following my arrest and imprisonment for accessing illegal Internet pornographic images of females under eighteen years of age, I had begun to regain my spiritual focus. Nevertheless, there were still many days when the deadweight of sorrow, guilt, and failure would overmaster my spirit and deliver an engulfment of dismal hopelessness to my soul. There was a recurrent sense of distress concerning all of the loved ones and friends I had let down, not to mention the fact that I had altogether fallen short of honoring God and the call to ministry He placed on my life.

During that hot July summer of 2006 inside a Texas prison, I received a letter from my pastor. This is what he had written:

Dear John,

I know that your remorse for what you have done is eating you up. I know that the result of an immoral lifestyle is a scarred life that makes it difficult to just have a normal life. I know it is hard, but I know that God is all-powerful and He can give you grace to overcome, to forgive yourself, and to live a life that glorifies Him. I have the utmost faith in you; that if you will stay true to the Word of God and do what you know to do, you will not fall back into the trap that is baited for you. The bait will not go away, the bait will only get more attractive. The bait will always call your name, just remember that Jesus calls your name too: *"My sheep hear my voice, and I know them, and they follow me."* (John 10:27)

I hope that you will have a great day today, we are praying for you. More later. With love and prayers,

John B. Bryant

That correspondence was a much needed source of encouragement, and I hope you will be encouraged by it too. As I read that letter, there were certain words that especially caught my attention:

"...the trap that is baited for you. The bait will not go away, the bait will only get more attractive. The bait will always call your name..." Those words so accurately portray the present and prevailing progression of sexual addiction as a "besetting" sin.

Sexual sin is a trap because it confines a person spiritually, mentally, emotionally, and even physically in such a way that, once a person is enmeshed within its clutch, it is extremely difficult to escape. Those who do escape are always scarred by the vice of sexual sin, and oftentimes find themselves less resistant to subsequent encounters with the "baited trap".

For the Christian who has escaped the trap of sexual sin, it is essential to remain mindful that the trap is always baited:

1.The bait will not go away!

> *"When the devil had finished tempting Jesus, he left him until the next opportunity came."*
> (Luke 4:13 [NLT])

Satan is always looking for opportunities to manipulate and provoke us to sin. Those temptations may come at interval occurrences, but when you least expect it the bait will appear. The bait has never actually gone away for good. The bait may unexpectedly emerge in different forms, so *always expect* the bait of sexual temptation to appear!

2. The bait will only get more attractive!

> *"I was looking out the window of my house one day and saw a simpleminded young man who lacked common sense. He was crossing the street near the house of an immoral woman. He was strolling down the path by*

> *her house at twilight, as the day was fading, as the dark of night set in. The woman approached him, dressed seductively and sly of heart...My bed is spread with colored sheets of finest linen imported from Egypt. I've perfumed my bed with myrrh, aloes and cinnamon. He followed her at once, like an ox going to slaughter or like a trapped stag awaiting the arrow that would pierce its heart. He was like a bird flying into a snare, little knowing it would cost him his life."*
> (Proverbs 7:6-10, 16, 17, 22, 23 [NLT])

When *opportunity* and *temptation* intersect with one another, the likelihood of giving in to sexual sin is vastly escalated. Satan is aware of this fact and uses it for exploiting and inciting our sinful nature in convergence with worldly influences. We live in an era when *opportunity* for engaging in any assortment of sexual misdeeds is more convenient and concealable than ever before in history. We also live in an age when worldly influences toward sexual depravity are presented with such amplified power of irresistible attraction that the temptation for "taking the bait" can more ably short-circuit a Christian's spiritual common sense and lead him into sinful compromise. Remember, the bait's attractiveness is a deceptive enticement embedded with piercing hooks which will drag you away to a place of death: (see *James 1:14-15*)

Sexual temptation presents the attractive bait;

The sexual addict takes the bait as compulsive preoccupation is incited within the mind;

The addict then manifests sexually immoral action through his external choices and behavior;

Death [ruptured and broken fellowship with God] is produced in the sexual addict's life.

Stop being deceived by the misleading attractiveness of the bait!

3. The bait will always call your name!

"So she seduced him with her pretty speech.
With her flattery she enticed him."
(Proverbs 7:21 [NLT])

The more we "listen" to the voice of worldly cultural relativism concerning sexual immorality, the more we let our guard down in the area of conforming to that sexual immorality. The world system uses an entirely different standard than Christians when it comes to defining the principles of right and wrong sexual behavior. The world defines sexual morality according to *cultural relativism*—that is, customary beliefs and social forms relating to right and wrong will drift in the direction of majority preference. Having said that, it is important to note that the majority preference of an ungodly society will inherently drift in the direction of moral degeneracy. To quote Pastor John B. Bryant, as published in the *Life in Unity* newsletter, January 27, 2006:

"In this world we find that immorality is rampant and is becoming the norm for what seems to be the majority. We know that disobedience to the Word of God is never acceptable; we know that it is vital that we stand upon truth!...[B]ut today we are finding it more and more distasteful to make a stand against the lifestyles that are promoted by our media and society."

The voice of cultural relativism, via media and ungodly societal trends, is a bait that is calling your name with the goal of luring you away into lower standards of holiness by offering your sinful nature the promise of special pleasure and advantage. Recognize this voice for what it is and do not be seduced and enticed by its destructive allurements!

JESUS CALLS YOUR NAME

The solution for avoiding the baited trap of sexual sin and the beguiling voice of our enemy is to stay true to the

Word of God. By doing this we remain perceptive to the voice of the Spirit of Christ Jesus who will lead us in the right direction from day to day if we are willing to continue following Him by staying true to the Word of God:

> *"My sheep hear my voice, and I know them, and **they follow me**."*
>
> (John 10:27)

> *"We do this by keeping our eyes on Jesus, on whom our faith depends from start to finish..."*
>
> (Hebrews 12:2 [NLT])

As I have heard Dr. David Jeremiah say: "The difference between faith and failure is focus." The four applications of practical holiness which are explained in chapters 6-9 of this book are designed to help us stay true to the Word of God and maintain our focus on Jesus Christ. It is so important to remember that *daily persistence* in practicing these practical applications is vital to the ongoing revival of God's active and operative Holy Spirit power in our lives.

What exactly does it mean to be *persistent*? It means to have a steady devotion to the same course, principles, disciplines, etc...:

> *"Therefore, my beloved brethren, be ye steadfast, unmoveable, always abounding in the work of the Lord, forasmuch as ye know that your labour is not in vain in the Lord."*
>
> (1 Corinthians 15:58)

I realize there will be days when it is simply impossible to give exclusive devotion to all four practical applications; however, we must honestly make every effort we can to maintain a *daily persistence* if we expect God to be persistent in supplying us with the necessary daily empowerment to escape sexual addiction.

Again, this is a transforming and renewing process. As part of that process there will be battles and resistance from your sinful nature. Sometimes the resistance may become so convulsive within your soul that you find yourself seemingly torn to shreds spiritually through the persistent practice of these practical applications of holiness. The reason is that the Holy Spirit power of God is uprooting and purging the many strongholds to which we have allowed our soul to conform. This transforming and renewing process is a type of "civil war" going on between the Holy Spirit and our sinful nature:

> *"The old sinful nature loves to do evil, which is just opposite of what the Holy Spirit wants. And the Spirit gives us desires that are opposite from what the sinful nature desires. These two forces are constantly fighting each other, and your choices are never free from this conflict."*
>
> (Galatians 5:17 [NLT])

As I travel the journey of transformation and renewing, the resistance of my sinful nature has often times been menacingly violent. For example, I have gone through battles where I literally ripped a Bible to pieces and gave away all of my study references, resolving that I was finished with Christianity because it is easier to just live according to the flesh. A few days later the smoke-filled battleground of my soul cleared, and God was standing there extending His hand saying, "Come on, John, get back up. Let's move forward."

> *"Though he fall, he shall not be utterly cast down: for the LORD upholdeth him with his hand."*
>
> (Psalm 37:24)

Don't give up when you encounter the fierce battle of resistance from your sinful nature. It is through these battles that we are educated and made stronger for the next round of spiritual combat. As Charles H. Spurgeon has so fittingly stated:

> "God knows that soldiers are only to be made in battle; they are not to be grown in peaceful times. We may grow the stuff of which soldiers are made; but warriors are really educated by the smell of powder, in the midst of whizzing bullets and roaring cannonades."

I just want you to expect that there will be resistance to the change that God's Holy Spirit is making as He renovates your soul by way of your daily persistence to the practical applications of holiness learned in this book. Recognize the resistance for what it is and don't "break weak". If you stumble, get back up. I assure you that with each successive battle, the landscape of your soul will be further transformed toward Christlikeness. Battle precedes victory; if you wish to experience victory, you must identify and utilize God's provisional "weapons of warfare" persistently.

My dad, Herschel "D" Brown, Jr., said something to me a couple of years before he went home to be with our Lord. I hope to never forget these words: "You can make it happen with persistence, discipline, and determination!"

Maintain your steadfast devotion to daily *persistence*, *discipline*, and *determination* in practicing the practical applications of holiness in this book and you will experience the ongoing revival of God's active and operative Holy Spirit power in your life. Eventually you will be able to look back and say, "Wow! God truly has refashioned my life in a way that no other power in the universe could possibly have done! Hallelujah! I have escaped the besetting sin of sexual addiction!"

A FINAL COMMENT

I hope you will re-read the second part of this book for the simple fact that repetition is the mother of skill. Then I hope you will very thoroughly study the *four applications of practical holiness* in chapters 6-9 for detonating the ongoing revival of God's active and operative Holy Spirit power in your life. Ask God to teach you how to master the implementation of these applications into your daily living.

Do not be discouraged if there are days or moments when you stumble in some area of thought or behavior along your journey toward sexual purity. Just get back up, run to God, identify what ways you may not have been thoroughly practicing the four applications of practical holiness in this book, and make the necessary course corrective:

> *"[The godly] may trip seven times, but each time they will rise again..."*
>
> (Proverbs 24:16 [NLT] brackets mine)

If this book has ministered to your soul, I would like to ask you to keep its message alive by getting it into the hands of someone else who would benefit from reading it as well. Please let them read your copy or direct them to where they may obtain a copy of their own. (Toll-free 877-BUY-BOOK, or on the web at www.buybooksontheweb.com) Either way, I ask for your help in spreading the message of deliverance found within the pages of this book.

I believe this book will serve as a great resource for pastors who wish to provide practical information to those they counsel who battle compulsive sexual issues. Will you let your pastor know about this book? If you are a pastor, will you let other pastors know that this book is available?

Oh, how I pray that this book has ministered to your soul. I love you in the Lord and want you to know that I am praying for you. I may or may not know your name, but God does. As you have read this book, you have been in my prayers. May I request that you keep me in your prayers as well? Thank you...

John Allen Brown
(Romans 15:13)